To my beloved husband, I thank you for your willingness and boldness to declare 'whatever it takes' to love the Lord. As your wife, to watch you live this declaration every day has been life's greatest testimony for me of God's love, grace and acceptance of who we are in Him.

My hope is that whoever may have a chance to read Johns journey with the Lord will see a glimpse of hope and receive a revelation of God's love.

Clare Davidson
Wife and Partner

John has a gift for communicating God's truth and love with illustrations that penetrate the heart and capture the imagination. His hunger for intimacy with the Lord and his desire to bring others into an awareness of who they are as sons and daughters of Father God saturates all that he teaches and writes. I praise God that he is a part of our ministry school and my life.

Pastor Shawna Diehl
New Life Christian Fellowship

Great Lakes Supernatural Ministry School
Founder

My dad has always been there for me. He's one of a kind. He's that great loving father figure in my life, and I am truly blessed. As time passes by, we all do our share of growing up, both of us. We have learned from our mistakes, and taken on each experience as a great life lesson learned.

Fortunately for myself, I have a dad who is there for me 24/7, always there with a positive word of knowledge from the Bible. He keeps me strong. To this day, I look at my dad and I can say that I see the love of the Father. I'm proud of my dad. He's encouraging and it's inspiring to me to come home to a joyful household in which I can hear praise and worship at all hours of the day and night. I know I can either find my dad singing in the basement, pouring his heart out to God or reading the multiple passages in the bible, in order to reach out with uplifting words to others around him. I can see how much love he has for my mom, my brother, and myself.

Knowing that I won't go a day without a hug or kiss on the forehead is a warm heartfelt feeling I'm fortunate to have. I'm blessed to have such a wonderful family, and to have a smart encouraging dad to guide me in my life tribulations.

Thank you Papa Bear,
I Love You

Rachael Lynn Davidson
Loving Daughter Baby Bear

John reveals Gods work in his heart, after his declaration of "whatever it takes" .This book is for those whose heart echo's John's cry, "God I want more of you" Join with John in his adventure with our heavenly vinedresser as God cuts away all that stands between Him and us. Jesus words of John 15:1-17 come alive in the pages of this book as The Godhead prepares our hearts to be His Dwelling Place and His glory revealed.

Blessed of God,
Vicki Krupiczewicz –Servant of the Living God

The Angel and the Vision

A Revelation of

Love

and Grace

John M. Davidson

Scripture quotation marked (KJV) are from the King James version of the Bible.

Scripture quotations marked (NKJV) are from the New King James version, © 1979, 1980, 1982 by Thomas Nelson, Inc. Used by permission. All rights reserved.

Scripture quotations marked (NIV) are from the Holy Bible, New International Version, ©1973, 1978, 1984 by the International Bible Society. Used by permission

Scripture quotation marked (NKJV) are taken from the New King James Version. Copyright © 1982 by Thomas Nelson, Inc. Used by permission. All rights reserved.

Scripture taken from *The Message*. Copyright © 1993, 1994, 1995, 1996, 2000, 2001, 2002. Used by permission of NavPress Publishing Group."

Take note that the name satan and related names are not capitalized unless they start the beginning of a sentence. We choose not to acknowledge him even to the point of violating grammatical rules.

THE ANGEL AND THE VISION A Revelation of Love and Grace

For speaking engagements you may contact the author at:

John M. Davidson
Casa Royale Ministries
3804 Michael Ave SW
Wyoming, Mi 49509
e-mail; supernaturalroyalty@gmail.com

ISBN: 978-0-557-72000
Printed in the United States of America
©2011 by John M. Davidson

Library of Congress cataloging-in-Publication Data (pending)

No part of this book may be reproduced or transmitted in any form or by any means, electronic or mechanical, including photocopying, recording, or by any information storage and retrieval system without permission in writing from the publisher.

This book is lovingly dedicated to my most awesome wife,

Clare Davidson

Her tenacious spirit and undying love has been a rudder pointing me to passionate relationship with God. She has stuck by me through thick and thin; good times and bad and I am proud to call her my partner and wife. Like myself, Clare has had visions of God's love that have shown us that true love is a choice and a revelation. Thank you for choosing to love me and to be open to God to see a revelation of His amazing love.

Table of Contents

		Introduction	11
Chapter	1	The Beginning	17
Chapter	2	The Angel and the Vision Part 1	73
		Part I Form of Godliness	77
		The Angel and the Vision Part 2	78
Chapter	3	The Fog	87
Chapter	4	The Tread Wheel	107
Chapter	5	The Storage Room	113
Chapter	6	The Prophets	119
Chapter	7	The Youth Room	123
Chapter	8	The Infirmary	131
Chapter	9	The Worshippers	137
Chapter	10	The Board Room	144
Chapter	11	A Comfortable Church	151
Chapter	12	A Pierced Heart	161

Acknowledgements

A book like this would never have been possible without the input and involvement of a myriad of people in my life. I would not be here today without my wife of almost 23 years. My favorite part of the day is the morning where we usually can be found in the living room drinking fresh cups of coffee as we share about all aspects of our lives; our hopes, dreams, visions, children and work. I can honestly say I love Clare more now than ever and I know she would say the same. The experiences of *The Angel and the Vision* and *The Dwelling Place* have made that all the more real.

I will be forever grateful to Ed Kerkstra who I affectionately call Father. He spent hundreds of hours praying with me. Without his tireless and patient work of teaching me to hear the voice of the Lord, I would not have been able to receive this amazing vision, nor write this incredible story of God's love. I cannot say enough about this man. All I can say is that I have learned to see, feel and hear the voice and the love of God in a way I never thought possible.

And then there is Vicki Krupiczewicz who pushed me beyond my comfort zone to fulfill the call of God on my life. She has been like iron sharpening iron as she challenged me to pursue my heart cry of "Whatever it takes". She is a true prophet of God who is not afraid to speak the truth. She was the inspiration for Lady Wisdom in this book and the one who gave me the input for the description of the fruit.

I am so thankful to the Pastors in my life who have poured themselves into me. For Pastor Randy Vruggink of River of God Church who personally disciple me and gave me a safe place to grow for six years.

Thank you Pastor Lonnie Shields of New Life Christian Fellowship, my home church, in Grand Rapids Michigan for never stop laughing. You make me smile. Your sound Bible teaching and passion to see the power of God flow in healing of body, soul and spirit have deeply imprinted this book. You and Pastor Jon Hazeltine are pioneers cutting a path through the jungle of religion to release a fresh light of the love of God.

And a big thank you to Pastor Shawna Diehl, my worship leader and founder of Great Lakes Supernatural Ministry School who taught me that Jesus is a fun person to be with and someone who loves to laugh. You taught and demonstrated "drinking in the Spirit" in the most undignified way that cut through the fog of religion that shrouded my life for so long.

I am very grateful to Judy Avery who spent an enormous amount of time helping me to edit this book.

I could mention so many others but suffice it to say none of us can reach our destiny without linking our arms and pouring out ourselves to one another with God's love

The
Angel and the Vision

By John M. Davidson

I saw a vision of an angel who had a message. A message revealed to my heart as I cried out to God that I wanted Him more than anything- whatever the cost, whatever it takes.

I wanted to be a man of faith who trusted God without doubting. I wanted my whole vision to be filled with His love. I found that one must be careful what one wishes for…. the results just might be life changing!

Introduction

Jesus said that He came to give life and to give it more abundantly. This story and vision is about that journey to freedom of becoming liberated from selfishness so that one can fulfill the call on their life. It is about a journey into intimacy. For me it was becoming more and more aware of the presence of God and the journey I took to get there. It is a visualization that brings light to the darkness; a darkness that is so set on stealing my true destiny.

It is a revelation that sets my captive heart free, drives out the demons and heals the sickness within...but I had to first let God do that to me and in me.. It had to first come from intimacy with God. There was the part about seeing things dimly at first, maybe even distorted and then slowly coming to the "knowledge of the truth". This journey and progression goes from believing lies and ends up with being delivered from darkness to light.

The vision starts in darkness but ends in glorious light, hope and joy. It starts with discerning a world system and demonic enemy that seem to be in control but as the story progresses I find they get smaller and smaller until they are insignificant and Emmanuel becomes my Lord and best friend.

The Angel and the Vision

In 1 Corinthians 14:3 it says "that everyone who prophesies speaks to men for their strengthening, encouragement and comfort." It goes on to say in verse 8 that when you prophesy, it is to edify the church. My desire in releasing this is that it will truly edify and build up the church. This is not about laying heavy burdens on the Church. The world, the flesh and the devil have already done a good job of that.

I have come to a deep realization that when God presents truth in a strong way it is always supported by His amazing love and grace. So if there is a prayer to pray, here it is, "that people will be strengthened, encouraged and comforted by this amazing prophetic vision." It says in 1 Corinthians 13 that we see in part and we prophecy in part. God reveals things to us in pictures that help His truth be more easily understood. He works through our personalities, talents and even our experiences.

I see things best in pictures. For me this was a blueprint to escape the horrible maze of confusion I was in for decades. I was one who grew up in a very religious home where God was seen as a fiery God of judgment, but not a God of love. He was not someone fun or someone whom you could be intimate or relax with. To me it was all about the rules. I got so involved in being religious that I became thick skinned and dense headed.

> I wanted to see what I needed to believe

It got to the point after beating my head against the wall for decades that I became sick of religious cliques, and lukewarm attempts to appease God. At the same time I found I was hating myself for being in this miserable lifestyle. I began looking at the Bible and saw that if Jesus claimed to give life and give it more abundantly, then that is what I wanted. I desired it all and I wanted it straight. I wanted to cut through the lies and get to the raw truth.

The Angel and the Vision

I wanted to see what I needed to believe. I found that it is in the midst of seeing and hearing the deep things of God, of understanding deep mysteries and knowledge, and of learning to walk with a faith that can move mountains, that everything must be encapsulated and saturated with God's love actively at work in us... or it means nothing. I saw that if Jesus claimed to give life and give it more abundantly, then that is what I wanted. I wanted it all and I wanted it straight. Let's cut through the lies and get to the raw truth. I wanted to see what I needed to believe.

So I began to learn about being patient and kind with each other, not envying or boasting, not rude or self-seeking, not easily angered or keeping a record of wrong doing, not delighting in evil, but rejoice in the truth; always protecting, trusting, hoping and persevering; never failing each other; and by doing that learning to quickly forgive.

As a body we need each other. We are to be knit together in love. This is where it's at but how to internalize it?

So let us see who the real enemy is.... it is not each other; it is the devil with his principalities and powers who seek to devour and divide us as individuals and church. It is a worldly system that caters to the lust of the eyes and flesh and the pride in one's possessions. It is the battle of allowing ourselves to be dominated, manipulated and controlled by the devil and His system or to be set free, loved and led by the Lord. It is a battle to being set free from the demons of our own mind; of having lived and thought a certain mindset for years of being tortured by that mindset. It is in refusing to put the old man to death instead of choosing life. Let us see who really loves us and passionately wants to have a deep and satisfying relationship with us. We need to regroup and fight for the victory that is ours in Christ Jesus!

1

THE BEGINNING

Excitement was in the air. It was Christmas Eve! Outside the snow danced and swirled as it cascaded down from a bluish gray sky. The weather had been up and down lately with its usual thaws and freezes. Michigan was known for these extremes as it gathered up steam for a long, cold winter. My brother, Rick, who was four years older than I, was quite agitated and excited to have us view the eighth wonder of the world that was rapidly growing from the eve of our two story rental house on Union Street. We were bundled to the nines to weather the blustery chill and stood gazing in wonder at this glistening feat of nature.

A huge icicle had formed off the edge of the inner eave of the second story and was already firmly attached to the ground. It was larger than the body of a grown man, although much

The Angel and the Vision

more twisted and gnarled at the top, and had the appearance of something quite magical out of Disneyland. Where the icicle touched the ground, it resembled something like tree roots where the stalagmite had joined the stalactite and now had melted into the ground creating a pool of sheer ice.

At the roof line, yellow hues of maple syrup brown had intertwined with the icy whiteness from the decayed oak leaves. Just months earlier, the leaves which had blown off the massive oak trees that overshadowed the roof, had settled in the lower parts of the valley on the roof. The fall rains had matted down the leaves in the roof's valley now released their permanent dyed colors which now streamed its way down the frozen mass. Each thaw had sent new layers of colored water to trickle down and refreeze to create its gargantuan size. It truly was a sight to behold.

"Stand back Johnny," Rick said authoritatively. If that breaks and falls it will crush you like a bug. I took a quick step back looking up in apprehension and deep wonder at this amazing feat of nature. It really did look huge. I sucked in a deep breath of winter air and exhaled slowly watching a dreamy breath of frosted air curl lazily through the new frigid atmosphere.

The ground crunched begrudgingly beneath my zippered rubber boots as I retreated to a safe distance. Rubbing my hands together I tugged on my handmade mittens to create some friction and made a tight fist to keep my hands warm.

While rocking back and forth on the balls of my feet and simultaneously blowing on my gloves for warmth, I felt a tug across my back, but under my coat that reminded me that Mom had made these mittens with the design that they would never

The Beginning

be parted from each other. A braided string connected the two mittens which tracked down both arms of the jacket and across the back. Mom was not one to be trifled with when it came to matching up mittens and socks. If there was any way to connect them she would find a way.

I stood motionless as Rick picked up a broken icicle and threw it at the bigger ice monstrosity. "We need to test it, Johnny to make sure it won't fall down," Rick explained wisely. I watched as my older brother, Rick continued to test out his Einstein theory by throwing snow balls and icicles at the big ice pillar. "Looks like its ok" Rick replied with a sigh of relief. It isn't coming down anytime soon."

After awhile, I began to get bored and began pleading with my brother to go inside. By now the bone-chilling cold was sending shivers down my spine and my teeth chattered behind my bluish red lips. I rubbed the back of my hand across my dripping nose and then whipped it on my sleeve. "Come on Rick, let's go." I pleaded tugging his coat. I glanced at the residue left on my arm and tried to brush it off. "Come on," I pleaded again with greater force, tugging a little harder this time. "It's freeeeezing out here!"

Rolling his eyes, Rick finally relented and we headed inside unbundling ourselves from our layers of coats and sweaters and began playing with tinker toys.

Tinker toys were the prehistoric version of Legos. They were straight sticks about twelve inches long and of various colors that fit into a donut shaped piece of wood with holes drilled in various positions. You could make some cool designs and this challenged both of our creative little minds.

The Angel and the Vision

I watched as Mother busied herself with Jimmy in his crib. Jimmy was a year and a half younger than I. I guess that would make him about two and a half years old. He was very, very sick and had been diagnosed with some kind of disease called leukemia. I didn't know much about it, but you could tell he was in a lot of pain and his stomach had ballooned up to size of a woman carrying a baby full term. I didn't know about all that. I just knew that we had to be very quiet all the time and mom seemed to spend all her time taking care of him. I didn't understand it at all.

Now I was one of those hyper-active kids who was always on the go and needed mammoth amounts of attention. In today's age, I would have been labeled ADD and would have probably been pumped full of Ritalin, but at that time, I was just viewed as a serious pain in the butt.

"Look Mommy," I beamed as I held up my tinker toy contraption. When I got no response, I kept tugging on her dress. "Look Mommy, look what I made," I said more insistently.

"I'm busy, son, I can't give you attention right now. Jimmy needs my help."

Not to be undaunted I continued to pester her for attention. "Look, look mommy."

Grabbing me by the arm Mother looked fiercely into my eyes while shaking me and said, "STOP! Can't you see that I'm busy?" She looked me firmly in the eye as our eyes locked in a challenge of wills. Her eyes contained a fierceness that defied one to challenge her.

The Beginning

My arm stung from where her sharp, long finger nails had dug deep into the fleshy part of my arm. I rubbed my arm gingerly as if trying to remove the slightly bleeding nail marks. I hung my head and went back to my tinker toys. My eyes blurred from the red hot tears that hung precariously on my lower eyelids. I felt frustrated and my little wounded spirit quivered in pain. I just wanted someone to pay attention to me.

Somewhere in the midst of this an idea began to grow in my mind like a tiger lily unfolding in the morning sun. It was because of Jimmy. It was because of him that Mother doesn't have time for me. Slowly this little thought became an idea, and I began to plot and scheme. "If I can get rid of Jimmy somehow, then she will pay attention to me."

I found myself rationalizing a strategy from an anguished heart as my four year old mind worked overtime to create a masterful plan. Mischievousness was in full throttle and a small seed of anger began to grow in my little heart. The more I played with my tinker toys, the more I thought about how my younger brother was getting all the attention and that just fed the fire. Like a raging wave that was twisting towards the ocean shore, my anger finally crested and I slammed my tinker toy creation on the floor watching it break into a thousand pieces.

"It isn't fair," I fumed with a grunt of aggravation. I bit my quivering lower lip as the tears that had been held back for so long scalded my hand as they cascaded off my tiny cheeks.

Grabbing the biggest piece of tinker toy that had not come apart from my tantrum, I got up and stealthily began making my way over to Jimmy's room. A plan was quickly formulating in

The Angel and the Vision

my creative mind that I was sure would solve everything. I clutched the shaft of the tinker toy and examined the round wooden head that was crammed onto the stick.

"This would work very nicely," I thought with gleeful satisfaction. As I tiptoed towards the bedroom, I looked furtively into the kitchen to see Mothers back turned to me. She was busy washing dishes and did not notice my stealthy movements and that was all the encouragement I needed. Reaching the door, I snuck in like a panther cat on the prowl. Jimmy was sleeping in his crib, totally oblivious to the entire drama unfolding around him.

Finding a foot stool, I quietly dragged it over to the crib so I could grab the side bars of his crib and reach between them. With covertness like precision, I raised my hand with the tinker toy weapon in a cocked position and came crashing down with as much force as a four year old could muster, whacking Jimmy square on his forehead. Quick as Jack flash, I was off the stool and back in the living room playing tinker toys like nothing had happened. Already at this young age I was fast learning the art of misdirection and shifted blame.

Jimmy's eyes flashed wide opened with frightened surprise, and for a moment the pain did not seem to register in his fevered, cancer ridden body. However, pain is pain, and suddenly, a moose sounding bellow came from the depths of his little lungs. He was screaming to high heaven. Mother went flying from the kitchen to see what the ruckus was all about. She gathered up Jimmy who was hysterically crying his eyes out and began cooing and stroking him, rocking him back and forth while simultaneously doing her detective work to get to the

The Beginning

bottom of this. The initial red welt that had been measured out in great precision was fast growing into a nice size knot right in the middle of his forehead.

"Alright, who is responsible for this?" Mom demanded. Her eyes darted back and forth between my brother and me. Rick piped up before I could get a word out edgewise. Obviously he did not want to get blamed for this one, and I got the impression I had done similar things to him before.

"It wasn't me. Johnny is mad at Jimmy because he thinks you are giving him too much attention. He just went in there and wacked Jimmy on the head with a tinker toy." Rick gave me a wan even smile that hinted of a Cheshire cat, but not enough to get him into equal trouble. I caught the slight smirk on his face of "I got you back this time; you're going to get it now look."

I felt the flush of dismay creep up the back of my neck and my cheeks started to burn from the rush of blood as I saw a flash of anger flit across mother's eyes. It was the kind of anger that made you think "run!" My eyes widened as big as saucers at being discovered. I did a gymnastic roll sideways and was up on my feet in point four seconds. I had been undone and I started my sprint for deep cover.

Faster than a lizard catching a fly with his tongue, Mother put Jimmy down with one hand and grabbed my arm with the other putting me into her famous vice grip; it was the kind of dig into your arm with the fingernails routine. I never even knew what was coming as my feet were moving in a fast sprint but I was going nowhere. A numbing, searing pain was already traveling down my arm as her finger nails continued to dig in with vampire precision.

The Angel and the Vision

"You're going to get it this time," Mom hissed, as spit flew from her mouth. Her eyes darted frantically around the room looking for the proper tool of persuasion as she continued saying, "I've had enough from you young man." Grabbing the belt, which just happened to be conveniently nearby, she began to lay it on my little behind...smack...smack...smack!

Screaming in pain I did my best to get away, but her grip was way too tight. As I tried to dance away from the belt that was laying painful blows on my tender behind, she held me firmly with one hand while belting me soundly with the other. As she spanked I ran. The only direction I could go was in a circle because she had a firm clamp on one of my arms. We went around in a circle three to four times before she had spent enough energy and began to calm down. Speaking through labored breaths she said a sentence of words that would end up shaping my life for the next forty years.

> Son, because you hit your brother, you are not getting any Christmas presents this year

"Son, because you hit your brother, you are not getting any Christmas presents this year." Mom looked me straight in the eyes with nostrils flaring and her heavy breathing breaking the now deadly silent air.

My little legs trembled beneath the spent energy of an angry mom. Welts had already started to turn a bright red where the belt had missed its intended target. My legs smarted, but the pain of not getting any Christmas presents for a four year old was so much greater. "No Christmas presents!" I cried out.

"You heard me young man. Now go to your room." Mom pointed her boney finger in the direction of the bedrooms with

The Beginning

a glare that demanded instant obedience. Even though her heavy breathing had diminished, the fierce look of determination in her eyes defied anyone to challenge her decision. I was totally caught off guard by this new discipline. It was inconceivable! I ran to my room and plopped on my bed sobbing my eyes out.

It was Christmas Eve and all my hopes and expectations that had been built up over the year were gone in an instant. I had been dreaming of Christmas presents for so long and now it was all gone. For a long time I lay in a fetal position sucking my thumb. I cried and cried until I could shed tears no longer.

That evening, I watched as my bother Rick and Jimmy opened their presents. Jimmy got this really cool car dash with all the dials and knobs. It had a windshield with working wipers and batteries that made the dash light up. Rick got a really fancy authentic electric Lionel train track, the train and all the cars and cabooses with all kinds of different tracks and water towers and things to go with it.

I watched as Dad and Rick spent the whole night putting it together. It was an amazing beautiful train set. Several times I moved closer to see if I could help or play only to be told, "I'm sorry Johnny, but you don't get any Christmas presents this year. You were bad. There will be no presents for you. You can't play with your brother's toys either."

Mom was still real mad and when she was like that Dad knew better than to interfere. If he did, he would be in the dog house also. I watched from a distance as Rick excitedly hooked up the transformer; placed the train with its various cars on the track and gave it a test run. Toot! Tooooooooot. Rick opened a

The Angel and the Vision

little container and put a substance in the stack that made smoke come out. It was really cool! Boy, they were having so much fun! I wish I could play with them.

This sinking feeling of loneliness and rejection was fast setting its hooks in my heart.

I turned my attention to the car dash that Jimmy had stopped playing with. I edged over quietly so that I could take the wheel and make gunning noises.

"Rrrrrrrrrnnnnnnnnnn! Rrrnn Rrrnn," I said, pretending to drive the car as I turned the steering wheel back and forth. A smile began to cross my face as my imagination took over.

Mother saw what I was doing and reached over and smacked me on the back of the head saying, "I said no. I'm not going to tell you again." Stars exploded out my eyes and for a moment I thought I was seeing little birdies. "Go to your corner young man, and I am not going to tell you again….and stay there until I tell you." The steely cold look in her brown eyes sent me scampering to the familiar corner with a whimper.

As I sat down my shoulders slumped in dejection, I found myself beginning to ask some probing questions. "What had I done that had been so bad?"

My thoughts raced back over the day as best as a small child could to try and figure things out. "Why is mother always yelling at me? What's wrong with me?" The frustration on my face would have told the story to anyone who was even slightly observant.

The Beginning

I tried to remember what it felt like to be hugged or kissed or told that I was special. I just could not seem to remember. All I could remember was the constant spankings and disciplines and now this. It was all a shadowy blur. It just seemed that I couldn't do anything right. My little heart ached and seemed like it was ready to break into a thousand pieces.

Little did I know that my birth was the result of an unplanned pregnancy born to a young mother who just wanted to do her own thing. My current father had just got out of prison when he met my pregnant mother. In her desperation, mom had promised God that if He gave her a man who would love her and her two children she would serve Him her whole life. She made a deal with God and when my dad came along; she felt He had answered her prayers. He had adopted me at birth and also my older brother when he had married her. Jimmy was their first child born of that union.

I didn't understand the issues of being part of an unplanned pregnancy, and a reminder of someone she extremely disliked. I just remember that it was always my fault and I could never please mom. I would later look on this and be grateful that at least she didn't abort me even though that is what my Grandma insisted my mom should do. Mom told me later in life that social services had taken me away from the hospital at birth and placed me in Bethany Home for 30 days because she was so unstable. In the past few years before my birth, she had already tried to commit suicide three times and even now had little regard for her life. I would later thank God I was born in 1960. Otherwise, this story and I would all be a mute point.

The Angel and the Vision

I sat in the corner trembling with tears streaming in an unending cascade of sadness asking myself, "Why can't I do anything right?" I had no idea this was 1964 and that the consensus was that children should be seen and not heard, or if you got in my way, I'm going to beat the crap out of you. In those days there were no books on child rearing.

"Why did no one love me? Why could I not seem to please mother? What is wrong with me?" All these questions with no answers were swirling around inside my heard. It seemed to me that the only way to get attention was to act out my negative behavior or be bad. If I was mischievous or naughty, that got me attention.

I'm sure I was not consciously thinking these thoughts, but I know that subconsciously I was finding out very quickly that bad behavior was getting me the attention I so desperately wanted. It was counterproductive attention that would morph into many forms over the next forty-two years. Years of choosing the seeds of rejection, bitterness, anger, fear and lack of self esteem which had been planted in that hour would form hundreds of thousands of wrong beliefs that would find their beginnings in this single event.

As I sat in that corner, my little world seemed to grow smaller and smaller. I was so sad and all alone. My outburst earlier against my brother was long forgotten. The fact that I had instigated it was irrelevant. All I could see was my present pain. Did anyone love me? Would I ever feel the warmth of arms wrapped around drawing me close in loving embrace that left me feeling secure and loved? Yes, those eyes would haunt me for decades. Could I ever reach a point where my mom and

The Beginning

dad would be proud of me and not look at me with those angry accusing disappointing eyes?

A slow glimmer of anger was sparking in the bottom of my soul. A song was being formulated deep within my tiny heart from which I was the self proclaimed author. Slowly, it beat a message in my little heart which became louder and louder. It would end up slowly winding its gnarly tentacles into my heart until it became a snarl that was impenetrable.

"It isn't fair that you should taunt me. It isn't fair that you should treat me this way." Over and over the song played its catchy tune in my head. I layed down on the floor, curled up in a ball and eventually fell into a fitful sleep.

Less than three months later, Jimmy passed away from the cancer. With Jimmy gone, I thought I would get more attention, but Mom just seemed to get more and more agitated with me. Her temper got shorter and shorter until nothing I did was right and nothing seemed to please her. The spankings only got more frequent and worse, along with the verbal abuse and deep seated anger.

Just a few months after Jimmy's passing, I found myself being told that they couldn't take it any longer, and I would be spending a while at Bethany Christian home. I remember the day of being driven to Bethany. I was so scared and lonely.

For the next year, I found myself in a group home setting where I continued to act out through mischievousness and silliness to get attention and love. Every day I would look out the window wondering when Mom and Dad would pick me up, but they never showed. Even though I felt rejected and

The Angel and the Vision

unloved, I still wanted their love and their approval. I felt very insecure and lonely, among a myriad of other negative emotions, which caused me to wet the bed and suck my thumb. For some reason, sucking my thumb gave me a sense of comfort and security. Sucking my thumb was to my memory my first mental and emotional comfort. My mother breast fed all her children and it was one of the few times I ever felt close to my mother's heart. Mentally, it helped me reconnect with her on a fantasy level. Obviously, I was starving for that warm loving touch of a mother.

In those days if you wet the bed, the punishment was a spanking. Fortunately those laws have long since been changed in group and foster homes. The instrument of choice was a wooden paddle with holes in it. Each day I found myself facing punishment because I was not able to control my bladder. To this day, I can still picture the stern face and disappointment as they pulled back the covers and discovered the yellow stain.

I remember the humiliation and shame as they exposed me in front of the other kids. Part of the punishment was exposure. Perhaps the Bethany Home staff thought that if you felt ashamed of your behavior you would stop. Of course the other kids would laugh and giggle and make fun of me behind my back. And there was the fear. Fear of not belonging, the uncertainty of not knowing where I fit in and not feeling the touch of a loving embrace. There was also the fear of the paddle. It was designed to inflict maximum punishment and the hand that applied it was a big guy with strong arms. I would lay awake at night being afraid to go to sleep because I didn't want to wet the bed. I don't remember anyone ever holding me or telling me I was valuable or loved. I do remember hearing "no"

The Beginning

a lot. In fact, whether it was at home or in Bethany Home, that was the dominate word I heard growing up..."No! No! No you can't do that. I said NO!"

Somewhere near the end of my tenure there, I remember trying to run away. I was growing more and more hostile towards authority. My weapon of choice was to hold everyone at bay with a water hose that I used to sprayed down the front window. Everyone laughed, but when it all settled down and I was caught, Mr. Paddle and I were again properly reunited.

I do remember two bright spots at that time. The counselor who was assigned to me was very kind and taught me how to play checkers and spell Mississippi; the other was sliding down the big hill in the winter. Those were good times and I remember even periodic times growing up later that my family would go sledding. It was a bright spot that to this day makes me smile. I continued to suck my thumb until late in my young years. I remember mom trying to get me to quit by telling me that if I didn't stop I would look like Bugs Bunny with my front teeth sticking way out. It really didn't work all that well as I received more comfort from sucking my thumb than the fear of having buck teeth. Most discipline or correction that I received was designed to promote a sense of pain or loss. There was the attempt to make me afraid of losing something if I didn't stop. Psychologically, it seemed to just make me more fearful rather than curb my behavior.

There was not much to remember over the next few years except my 'favorite' spot seemed to be the principles' office. He seemed to have that same exact paddle that I had seen and experienced when I was in Bethany Home. He also appeared to

The Angel and the Vision

have the same disappointed and exasperated stern look as my parents. I continued to act out my negative behavior and was considered the class clown and instigator. Every teacher from the third through the sixth must have spent many a night pulling their hair out trying to figure out how to mentor me.

By the time I was thirteen, I was pretty much used to the daily whippings and varied other methods of torture designed to 'break down my will', and had hardened my heart to my parent's constant preaching. The problem with trying to break someone's will is that either you break it and crush their spirit, or they grow more and more stubborn until their will is as solid as titanium. Everyone in my world seemed to be trying new techniques of discipline to get me to comply. With my personality being so strong, I gravitated to the latter and just got more and more stubborn.

Because I was in a high octane 'religious atmosphere' without a loving nurturing environment, it only fueled my pride and rebellion. They often spanked me for those two attitudes, but I tended to justify my behavior because I saw no repentance for their own self righteousness and anger.

The disciplines I experienced at home and school were very similar. Besides the paddle at the principal's office, a favorite discipline technique was to draw a circle in the chalk board and you would have to put your nose in the circle on the chalk. You then stood there for ten to twenty minutes in the front of the class in this humiliating pose. Between home and school I spent hundreds of hours with my nose plastered to some imaginary spot on the wall. Those disciplines didn't seem to work very

The Beginning

well either. Whenever I did something wrong, Mom pulled out the Bible and spent the next half hour expounding my sin.

At this point, I was kind of mentally caught in the middle. Mom tried hard to teach me the dangers of sin. She tried valiantly to expound the principles and character one should live by. She tried hard to get me to do the right thing; to get me to conform. She had promised God to serve Him her whole life and God forbid she would fail. I must conform.

Christianity was not about relationship, it was about doing the right thing. At that time in my life I did not understand the difference. If you didn't do the right thing and repent you would face God at the judgment seat. The thought of "blood on my hands," everything burning up as wood, hay or stubble or worse yet, going to hell and or missing the rapture, had put an "unhealthy" fear of God in me. In fact, that was the plan. That was how it was taught in church; that was how my parents perceived it and I was forced to toe the line.

The plan was to scare you into "serving the Lord." One of mom's favorite verses was from the Proverbs, *"Spare the rod and spoil the child"*. I think mom changed the verse to "Liberally apply the rod because he is a spoiled child."

By the time I was eight, my parents were extremely involved in church. They pretty much opened the local Baptist church and brought us along. Mom was pretty sure that memorizing scripture was the key to my redemption. She enrolled us in AWANA and BMA (Bible Memory Association). We were in overdrive memorizing the Bible, and over a ten to twelve year period, I would commit to memory over fifteen hundred verses. Mom had figured it out that if we hid the scriptures in our heart

The Angel and the Vision

we would not sin. I think her idea of "hiding" and God's idea of "hiding" were two different things; she was also very involved in the Basic Youth Conference Seminars with Bill Gothard. She got special permission to enroll us at an earlier age than usually allowed. In fact, I'm pretty sure I was the youngest one there. These were conferences that hosted from three to five thousand people at a time. I spent my summers for ten consecutive years attending these seminars. My strongest memory of that teaching was a picture of God looking like this triangle with two hands coming out each side. He was holding a chisel in one hand and a hammer in the other. Dad was the hammer and Mom was the chisel. In my family it was the opposite; Mom was the hammer and Dad was the chisel and I was the diamond in the rough. If you really rebelled against your parents, the hammer would really come down and a big slice of the diamond would be cut off decreasing your potential. I did think about this a lot.

My conclusion to all of this would prove devastating for me later on in life as I would come to the conclusion that my chance to be effective for God had passed me by. I had been too rebellious and proud; mom and dad had hammered and chiseled too hard and all that was left was a teeny tiny little diamond. This greatly affected my self esteem and my self-worth as a person.

Besides the memorizing, mom would constantly open the Bible to expound her favorite topics. Mom's favorite scriptures would mirror the prophets of old on judgment and sin. I never remember her talking about the joys of worship or the wonder of God's goodness and love. It was always fear based, performance oriented and striving for perfection. Nothing I

The Beginning

ever did seemed to be good enough or even enough for that matter... If you somehow arrived to a higher plateau there was no praise. I had to work harder, strive more to please God...and with no physical contact of love except when being disciplined, this would prove to be devastating. As I look back now, I am convinced that a loving nurturing relationship surrounded with firm principles and rules would have solved ninety percent of my acting out and rebellion growing up.

And then there was the rapture. There was many a night I would wake up in a cold sweat thinking I had been left behind. I was sure the rapture had come and I would have to go underground to escape an evil empire. I would rush down stairs to check in on my parents or go to my sister's room to see if they were still there. If they were still there, I would let out a sigh of relief. I would confess all my sins to make sure nothing kept me from getting raptured. To some degree, it kept me out of a little bit of trouble. It was obedience out of fear. It was like she was trying to break me down and contain me by putting me in a cage. External restraints would do the trick and force me into submission.

It would take a long time for me to find out that the best kind of change is from the inside out. In the meantime, though, I was about to experience another wrinkle that would consume thousands of hours of thought, and shape my life in a destructive way.

This new wrinkle happened one day when I was at my school friend house. Tom was a classmate in my grade; a close friend and was bragging about something he had hidden up in his

The Angel and the Vision

room that he wanted to show me. He said it was a surprise and wouldn't tell me what it was.

When we got to his room, he gave me a wink and opened a secret compartment. He proceeded to bring out piles and piles of magazines of girls in lesser and lesser array of clothing. Now granted, a majority of what he had, barely rivaled what is now wall papered on Victoria Secrets glass windows at the mall and another large portion of the pictures would be what some would call "art". But, there was enough that was provocative.

For me, it was the intent of looking. The birds had flown over and I had given them a place to nest. It was not just something that I had seen in passing. I looked at it and went "Yeah!" A primal longing of lust began to rise within me. My innocence had been pierced and a whole new horizon opened up to me. My creative mind was suddenly bombarded with a new sensory perception, and I was mesmerized. Whatever I thought sex was in those formative years was never satisfied in these magazines, because I still was a virgin when I got married at the ripe old age of twenty three. Right up to the time I got married, I still had no clue what the mechanics of sex really were, so what I saw was really mild by today's standards. The emotion of lust was there though in those formative years and in God's eyes, lust is lust. It is the intent to think; Regardless, I lost my innocence in that moment and a new fantasy life began that had the same result as if I did know. This fast became an area of retreat and escape; a place I could go into my mind and enjoy a fantasy world and a source of comfort. This would be my new comfort.

The Beginning

The next few years were spent on a quest to satisfy my curiosity. Mom always told me that the opposite side of the coin of mischievousness was creativity. If I could ever get my life straightened around I could really be used of God. I had a vivid imagination and sought to get answers of this thing called "sex"; even if it meant coaxing my neighbor friends or sister to play doctor. Fortunately, my invitations were met with boxed ears rather than a show and tell. The truth was, I was living in rebellion and pride, and wanted to get back and hurt my parents for how they had hurt me. I figured that they had hurt me and my way at getting back at them was doing things that they preached at me not to do. Besides, I did not see them living what they themselves preached and it drove me up a wall that Mom never once admitted she was wrong. She would be yelling at us one minute, and then the phone would ring. When she'd answer that phone, her whole attitude would change and she would be counseling someone in a quiet tone like a switch had flipped. This standard of comparisons and criticism did not help my situation though. I did not realize this until much later; that I really only ended up hurting myself.

I did not understand that my safe haven and place of comfort was to be found in an intimate loving relationship with a loving heavenly father, a Holy Spirit who would encourage and comfort me, and a friend in Jesus who would always be there for me. For me the safe haven would be found in building caves, forts and snow tunnels where I could go and be alone and live in my fantasy world.

At age sixteen, I met a rather sophisticated girl at BMA camp who challenged me to kiss her. I gave her a kiss on the lips, but quickly found that her tongue had sneaked past my lips and was

The Angel and the Vision

exploring my mouth. I followed her queue and ending up sucking on her tonsils. I didn't know what to do. I was just following her lead, but it felt real good. The electric fire that raced throughout me got me really scared. I had lived so long in a fantasy land that this reality was more than I could handle. She told me later that week that I was quite experienced, and there was no way this was my first time. We continued to kiss often and deep that week, but by the Friday night dedication service, I had made a vow to never kiss another girl again until I got married (that became a very long seven years as I actually kept that promise to God).

I remember thinking that I had better stop kissing her because I didn't want her to get pregnant. Little did I know? I also remember seeing the face of my parents being totally angry and disappointed with me. There was this part of me that still wanted their approval and another part of me that was scared to death of breaking their laws lest I get punished.

I did gain some wisdom from this experience. I came to the conclusion that I did not want a baby from someone I was not married to (even though I didn't know how to facilitate that yet), and I found that it took only a few moments to become an expert at kissing.

During my teenage years, I continued to act out my anger, lack of self esteem and creativity by being mildly destructive. I'm glad now my parents never let me graduate from a pump action pellet gun to a 22 or a shot gun. My anger was escalating to the point where I was killing birds, squirrels and frogs just for fun and spite and (allegedly) the neighbor boy was "stung" by

The Beginning

bees as he mowed the grass on his riding lawn mower. I was in the weeds across the creek in the back yard shooting at... Birds?

More and more distance was happening between my parents and me. I hardly saw my brother Rick any more. He basically lived and worked at my Grandpa and Grandma's farm. I had two younger sisters, and although I don't remember much about them, I do remember us playing a lot of board games to pass the time. Our favorite was Monopoly and Life. We played one game of Monopoly for as long as a week, and would end up printing our own money to keep the game going.

I continued to resist most things that Mom set in front of me to make me toe the line. Mom began to get more and more sophisticated with her disciplines of me.

Since what Mom was doing wasn't getting the desired results. She reasoned that she might as well get creative and try some new disciplines. I know she was getting totally frustrated with me and at wits end on how to get me to "toe the line." My parents tried scaring me by driving me by the juvenile detention center several times and threatening to drop me off. That one scared me for a little while, but even that was only a temporary solution.

I loved fire so much that mom thought she would help me to stop playing with the stove by putting my finger in the fire on the gas stove. I guess this was to teach me not to play with fire. Good plan! I never ended up becoming an arsonist so maybe that one had some positive results. Unfortunately, that one wouldn't be considered humane in this century.

The Angel and the Vision

I probably spent the accumulation of a year with my nose glued to the kitchen wallpaper. My mom loved eagles and the wall paper in our house was papered with an eagle design. "Pick your eagle and plant your nose on it," mom would say angrily. That one didn't work either. I would just go into a fantasy mode. One of my fantasies was to be like an eagle and be free and fly high in the sky. I would be able to escape all the pain and anger that was down on earth. Of course the metal fly swatter, the dowel rod and wooden paddle were always other choice methods of discipline that I received and sometimes multiple times daily. It must have been hard to have a hyper ADD child without the Ritalin. I was never diagnosed as such, but I contained all the symptoms…or was it just the outflow of years of learned rejection, lack of physical love, acceptance, anger and fear.

Regardless, I would have to eventually come to a realization that I was responsible for my own choices. No matter how bad the environment or people, my negative behavior and actions could not be an excuse. However, at this point all I could see was it was everyone else's fault.

As I got older, I got into a bad habit of lying. I think part of it was pain avoidance, but it also was a sense of real victory if I could get "one over" on Mom or anyone in authority. I could exaggerate and tell the biggest of whopper stories. I actually got quite good at portraying an innocent face and telling a big fat lie. One day I raided the cookie jar. Mom caught me just after the act and accused me of stealing cookies because she thought she had heard the top of the glass cookie jar rattle. She ran out of the other room she was in and told me to raise my hands so she could check my pockets.

The Beginning

"I didn't take anything Mom," I said innocently. After emptying them all out, and looking in my mouth to see if any cookies were in there, she let me go. I could tell she was puzzled and frustrated because she was certain that she had heard the glass jar rattling. I turned the corner, opened my fist and tossed the crumpled cookie in my mouth. She forgot to check my hands, ha! The cookies were crumpled in both fists. How did I ever get away with that one? I'll never know, but I got a lot of pleasure out of getting away with it.

Normally though, I did not get away with things that easily. Whenever I got caught or disciplined, I would go to the front porch, turn on the little organ piano and sing away at the top of my voice the song I had written at four years old. "It isn't fair that you should taunt me, it isn't fair that you should treat me this way..." Over and over, I would sing it until I was told to shut up and turn it off.

This bad habit of lying got quite annoying to everyone. Now one thing you have to understand about mom; to her everything was black and white. She was so black and white that to us kids recollection we never remember mom ever admitting that she was wrong. She was simply convinced that she was always right. She was God's spokes person for the truth. If she got angry that was righteous anger. Since she was never wrong, then how could we be right? Her determination of things was the absolute truth and there was no convincing otherwise. Besides, she had a Bible verse to back every situation up. How could you ever argue with God? She was Mom, and we were the children. In fact we kids heard that same train of thought after we had teenagers. "I'm the parent, you're the child. You do as I say!" That kind of thinking made

The Angel and the Vision

her the winner and we were still the losers. There was just no way to win that argument. There was no dialogue or talking things out. There was no cognitive reasoning or working through problems to a solution. Her word was law and you were to simply obey.

In her mind and according to the Bible there would be no liars in heaven, so mom was going to make sure I passed the pearly gates even if she had to burn it out of me. I, on the other hand, got a kick out of riling her up. Knowing how much this drove her crazy, drove me to lie to her all the more. It sounds kind of devious, (and it was) but as this story develops it will all make sense. At least I felt I had some sort of control.

The new punishment for lying was unveiled one day with great fanfare. I came in the house and was caught lying about something. Mom called me into the kitchen and did the Vanna White display of a can of red hot chili pepper. "Do you see what I have here young man?" she said holding the can in one palm while displaying the contents with the other. She then said that she was going to put that red hot chili pepper in my mouth and I would have to hold it in. "We are going to burn that lying tongue out," Mom said. "This will teach you not to lie."

I stood in the middle of the floor in deep dismay with a mouth full of red hot chili pepper for thirty minutes as the powder seared its way through my swollen tongue. I flared my nose as rebellious tears streamed down my face.

"Do what you will, but I will not be broken," I resolved. So, I stood there in quiet defiance as red smoke drifted out of my ears. I think it took a good day for my tongue to come back to normal, and for me not to feel so thirsty.

The Beginning

Mom tried this method many times more, but it just made me stronger. I may have been sitting down on the outside but I was standing up on the inside. I was determined that even if she could bend me, I would not break. The only bad side effect is that to this day, I will not eat hot stuff." I wonder where that came from.

During my teenage years, there were several other things that dominated my fantasy thought life besides girls. One was in designing a railway car that would be hand operated and could help me escape far away from home…preferably to Canada. I was going to run away. I spent hours and hours dreaming up every possible design but it never really got it to the assembly stage. I dreamed of going down the tracks in my hand made car pushing the draw bar up and down to make the railroad car go. I saw myself avoiding the police by traveling at night. I would just disappear and never be seen again. I would finally have freedom.

The other fantasy was that I would be big and strong so that no one could pick on me. If I had big muscles, people would like me and respect me. I would be able to stand up to those big bullies that picked on me. That was my fantasy reality, so when the advertisement came which claimed that "if you got a Charles Atlas course, no one would be able to kick sand in your face," I ended up getting the course and trying the exercises, but I never really grew much muscle.

I never really felt confident in myself (probably because I was always told I was wrong) and after trying softball and basketball and being laughed at for my lack of coordination, I shied away from those sports. I did find myself becoming more

The Angel and the Vision

and angrier on the inside as I got older. Both my parents had real anger issues. My grandparents on my mom's side would scream at each other for a half hour at a time. To me, I was learning from them that this was the way to solve your problems and communicate when you have conflict.

Dedicating my life to Christ at age sixteen was a bit of a turning point. Mom instilled in me from as early as I could remember that I would be a missionary someday. I fought that because I thought she was saying that to just make herself look good, but deep down there was something drawing me to be something bigger than myself. Despite my pride and rebellion I still wanted my parent's approval. After I dedicated my life to Christ, I started turning away from my juvenile criminal behavior of shooting things, breaking things, or stealing candy and things. I began to start thinking more of the future and doing something with my life.

I ended up getting a paper route and working at my grandparent's farm. At the farm I was regulated to shoveling manure and baling hay for $1.00 per hour. I learned a good work ethic, but I was more of a dreamer and did not work very fast. Even though I look back now and have come to the conclusion I was a pretty hard worker, I was told often that I was lazy and a sluggard. A sluggard is someone who is worse than lazy. I was not the greatest at piling the hay bales on the wagon and more than once, Grandma would hit a wood chuck hole. The wagon would sway and I would come down with the load. My Grandparents never let me once operate a piece of machinery all the days of my life even though my brother Rick was driving a tractor when he was ten. This always bothered me and made me jealous and angry. It was the fact that they

The Beginning

didn't trust me which in itself probably spoke volumes about their lack of confidence in me. Who would have thought the day would come when I would own my own excavation company?

With all my growing up and spending four to five days a week in the church coupled with constant "religion" at home, I never drew the connection of having an intimate relationship with God. God loving me was a concept, not a relationship. In fact, I saw God the same way I saw my parents; unbending, angry and distant.

Memorizing scripture was an assignment, not a life changing event. Prayer was something you did, not someone you did it with. Character was something you developed, not the byproduct of an intimate relationship with Father God. I continued to have my stash of magazines in a secret compartment in the floor of my closet, and now in a secret spot in the hayloft at the farm.

Christianity was something you did, not someone you knew. It was a list of commandments or principles that you followed. I just couldn't grasp a loving caring God who loved me warmly and unconditionally. I could not touch him or feel Him. The magazines seemed to do that for me. However, it was a sweet and sour experience. I felt the comfort in the beginning, but then I experienced the guilt in the end. I found myself saying I would not look at the magazines anymore and would destroy them, or I would feel guilty about getting angry or fearful, so I would try hard not to do these things. In the midst of this, I saw God as mad and disappointed at me. I had failed Him. I was supposed to be a Christian; I would have to try harder. I had to measure up to His standard. In the midst of this I dared not

The Angel and the Vision

discuss any 'weaknesses' with my parents. They would only turn and use that against me at a different time. I tried praying harder and reading the Bible more. It just didn't help. All this time I pictured God on this big white throne waiting to judge me. His face was a white light and He was in this white robe. If I did get a minor victory, I never felt satisfaction because the bar would be set higher. Keep pushing, keep trying, and keep performing. I heard no affirming words or loving embraces. No one said "I love you and am proud of you." I was an unprofitable servant. You should have already known that. I was afraid to die; I was afraid to live.

Going to Prairie Bible Institute in Three Hills Alberta, Canada, was probably the best thing that ever happened to me. I had pretty much decided to become a missionary. Mom and Dad of course had picked the school for me. It was a mission school and cheap. They even drove up there and checked it all out for me. With the exchange rate it was affordable for me as I had to foot the whole bill.

I was afraid to die; I was afraid to live.

Prairie was a strict no nonsense school, and fit in with the strict structure I was used to growing up in. It had a very stringent guy/ girl policy, and you would get in deep trouble if you were caught fraternizing with the girls for more than a few seconds.

It was a controlled environment and in many ways that was good for me. It got me away from my parents and destructive friends. I began making new friends. These friends were people

The Beginning

who actually had a heart for God. I spent the next five years dedicated to the Word and ended up becoming a model student. By my junior year, I was the one who not only obeyed the 'laws', but also enforced it to those who didn't. This didn't make me very popular, but I was doing what was "right". This especially annoyed my sister who had a free for all spirit and attended Prairie for one year. She did not appreciate it at all or understand my rigid thinking on keeping the rules and she thoroughly enjoyed aggravating me as only a sister can. I guess the fruit doesn't fall far from the tree.

I was kind of like the Pharisees without the robe. Although there were vast improvements in my behavior and lifestyle; it was mostly driven by a need to look holy. My actions made me holy so I tried harder and harder. I also had to make others try harder and harder. It was a new form of controlling, manipulating and dominating others. I was becoming just like my mother, but I didn't even see it at the time.

I don't remember having any bad memories of Prairie except for the pain of a couple girls who broke my heart. When I would like a girl, I would fall deeply in "love" with them and they consumed my thinking. I look back now and realize I must have come across as very clingy and needy. These fantasy relationships obviously didn't last long.

It didn't take long to discover that I would rather be a Pastor than a missionary, so I spent my five years getting a Bachelor of Theology and a Bachelor of Religious Education with a Pastoral minor.

I remember a funny story of the time I came home after my second year. I desperately needed a car and my Dad loaned me

The Angel and the Vision

the small amount of money to get it. He told me to pay him back as soon as possible. We always had enough to eat and the necessities, but extra money was always scarce. I worked hard and within a month had the money to pay him back. If you gathered from my story growing up, Mom was the dominate parent in the home. Mom would only defer to dad as a last resort if you were really bad and would say in exasperation to "wait till your fathers gets home to spank you routine." I had been learning in college that there was a chain of command and mom really wasn't the hammer...dad was. I was ready to pay back dad, but I made the mistake of mentioning to mom that I had the money to give to dad.

"Give it to me son, I'll take it," Mom stated emphatically.

I gave mom a cautious look and replied hesitantly, "Ahhhh, dad told me to give it him. I had better do what he says," Now I wasn't trying to be disrespectful to mom. There was a proper way to do things and I was following orders.

Anger sparked in her dark brown eyes, though. Stomping her foot, she raised her voice and said, "Get to you room right now." I knew that familiar tone and scampered up to my room. My first thought was how ridiculous this was as I was now twenty years old.

"I'm an adult now, why am I being treated like a kid," I pondered with a deep perplexity. I had learned a few things about honoring parents so I went along with it.

As I lay on my bed perplexed by the unfolding events, I heard the banging and slamming of cupboard doors as kitchen utensils were sent flying. Mom was talking to herself at different ranges

The Beginning

of decibels, but there was nobody there to listen. After what seemed like an eternity, I heard the familiar stomping up the stairs as Mom approached my room. Turning the knob, the door flung open and there she was standing larger than life, eyes wide and nose flaring with a wire fly swatter in her hand ready to give me my just punishment.

A great struggle of anger reflected in her eyes and she hesitated for just a moment. I just sat there half propped up on the bed calmly gazing at her. Suddenly, a brilliant thought popped into my head and without even thinking about it, I spoke out quite clearly while looking serenely into her eyes, "Father forgive her, she doesn't know what she's doing."

For a moment she stood there stunned, the fly swatter frozen in an elevated attack mode ready to inflict its pain. In that millisecond of time, time stood still with a deafening silence. A look of exasperated surprise suddenly flashed across her face. Stomping her feet, she pointed at me sputtering; "Get out of my house and stay out!" The funny thing was that I was dead serious and quiet when I said it, but for the first time I had stood up to her without being afraid.

I genuinely was feeling a compassion for her and was asking God to forgive her for she really was not acting in her right mind. She had given me a piece of her mind she couldn't afford to lose; besides that was no way to treat a twenty year old Bible school student. I only wish I had known how to act that calm towards her every time in the future. This time though, was certainly one for the ages.

I left the house and walked the streets for the next few hours until my dad came home and tracked me down.

The Angel and the Vision

"You probably should have given it to her son," Dad said with a chuckle. She was really mad. She is still stomping around the house.

"I was just trying to do things in the right way," I replied sadly. "Why does Mom have to act that way," I looked up into Dad's eyes hoping for answers. Dad didn't answer that directly, but just walked with me for a bit. "Why don't we hang out for a while until your mother cools down," he said smiling in a way that reassured me. "Once she calms down, she will be OK!"

I'll never forget that kindness. It was times like this that actually helped me to understand the goodness and mercy of God as I grew older. It helped me to grab hold and get a clear picture of the love of God. It reminded me of another time when I was much younger when Mom had told me that I was going to have to face my father when he got home. Something I had done had really aggravated her. When Dad got home and it was all explained to him, he came up the stairs to my room to mete out the punishment. I remember how he hated that. He hated to come home and listen to Mom be all exasperated at our behavior and then have her put him in a position where he had to discipline us. I can still see the sad look and deep sigh as his shoulders slumped. He worked in a factory that paid him by the piece. He would count and examine thousands and thousands of pieces a day for defects. He was one of the hardest workers, and would usually come home bone tired. He was so good at his job that they would clock him to set the rates. Disciplining us was a different matter and did not create a highlight in his mind. Mom was not one to be denied though. Discipline must be administered.

The Beginning

I had a few minutes of time to prepare for this situation and had already put on three to four extra pair of underwear. I was already sitting on my bed upstairs wringing my hands and holding my breath in anguished anticipation. I heard Dad trudging up the stairs and knock on my door. Dad came in and proceeded to tell me this was really going to hurt, but then he gave me a wink and a nod. "You better let your mother know how serious a spanking I am giving you," Dad said earnestly. "You know she can hear every little sound down stairs."

Mom had the sharpest ears and could hear you snap a twig a mile away. I was also positive she had eyes in the back of her head. There were so many times she caught me doing something and she wasn't even looking. Suddenly, I realized that this was that one of that rare occasion when he was on my side. He raised the belt and came down on my backside. He did it in such a way though that it made a loud slapping noise, but didn't hurt at all. I quickly caught on and howled in pain even though he had hardly hit me. Dad "spanked" me until he felt justice (mom) had been served. I cried up a storm and made it sound like the end of the world. Dad had served justice because mom was insistent that I needed a spanking, and I had received mercy, because Dad felt it was undeserving. He had created peace in an impossible situation. I'm sure I was wrong about something in this situation and perhaps Mom's idea of punishment was a little over the top. I got to see a picture of how God often does not treat us the way we deserve. I would never forget that.

With school ending I got a call to pastor a small Baptist church in Turtle Ford, Saskatchewan. The town was only about five hundred people, but over one hundred of them went to the

The Angel and the Vision

church. I had met a girl in my fourth year at Prairie Bible Institute; we had dated and somehow, got engaged even with all the restrictions. We ended up getting married just one month out of school, and I became the pastor three weeks later. I wish I could say that everything was hunky dory, but that was far from the case. Mom still saw me as a little kid, and had a hard time thinking of me as an adult or someone that possibly might have grown up. Even though we were a thousand miles apart, the telephone made things seem as if they were next door. Mom thought it was her duty to tell my future wife and parents every evil event of my childhood. I think she thought she was doing them and me a favor. It would turn out to be the unraveling of our marriage as it placed unnecessary doubts in their minds. God had done an amazing amount of change in me and I was trying to push ahead, but they were dredging up my past failures.

There was much tension about how the wedding should be planned which caused great offense in my parents-in-law. They were paying for everything and ninety eight percent of the guests were her family. However, my mom wanted equal say in how things should be. I remember this caused great aggravation in my wife and parents- in-law. I remember us agonizing over who I was to acknowledge as to who had made this all possible. We could not think of one compliment we could give to Mom; it was that bad. I probably should have thought harder and given one anyway. The problem was that as much lying I did in my teens; now I had swung to the far other extreme, and couldn't tell a lie if my life depended on it. This was probably to the exclusion of some other character attributes that could have been used in this situation.

The Beginning

We held our breaths during the ceremony. Would she stand up and object? During the toast, I complimented her mom on planning a wonderful wedding. Within five minutes of finishing the toast, my mom was chasing me down trying to make a scene. I was walking my way through the crowd as fast as I could to get away. She was furious that I had not said anything about her. My brother fortunately intercepted, and walked her permanently outside and away from the wedding party. Carolyn's family was huge on showing appearances, and this did not go over well. I tried my best to save face for them.

The wedding was over soon enough and we were off for a quick honeymoon. Within three weeks we were in our new parsonage with our meager belongings. Before you knew it, Sunday morning had arrived and I was ready to preach my first sermon.

Tension was in the air. The head deacon was holding several sheets of paper in his hand. The frustration on his face was evident to me as he looked bewildered at the outline before him. "What is this?" Mr. Bloom said. Mr. Bloom and his brother were farmers of over one thousand acres of land and pretty much ran the church. They had been there since it opened.

"Those are my sermons for the next year," I piped up proudly. I had figured I would cover church doctrine and preach on it for a whole year. I was so proud of it as everything lined up. All the words rhymed or started with the same letter, and I was quite excited to get into the meat of this deep theology.

Mr. Bloom handed me the outline back shaking his head in bewilderment, "I don't even want to know what you're

The Angel and the Vision

preaching on tomorrow!" he said emphatically. I gave him a quizzical look and walked away.

"What's up with him, I wondered." I just didn't get it that country folks were not that interested in dry theology. Especially if I was going to tell them how things should be run. Thus, was the beginning of my first week in a town, whose claim to fame was the largest cast turtle.

I ended up plowing through my dry, dusty sermons on the 'doctrine of the church' for a good six months. It took me a while to realize I was not in a school setting anymore and they needed something that would give them life. They needed something that related to their daily life. The Christian walk and experience was still mostly academic to me.

The people of the church were determined to get their money's worth out of me though, and before you knew it I was pretty much running everything and doing everything. I was a new John who was all pretty, polished, and disciplined. I threw my heart into my work with a vengeance. I was doing the work of the ministry and I had found my next 'comfort' zone. Although I was virtually required to do everything, I knew even at this young age that this wasn't right, and proceeded to begin to slowly change things. This was not without serious repercussions.

I remember one Sunday morning I asked one of the deacons to pray during the service. Boy, I really got chewed out for that. The lady who made the comment said, "We don't want to hear the deacon pray, we want to hear you pray!" I found out quickly that they did not like choruses either or me playing guitar. It had to be all hymns and organ. I loved choruses and

The Beginning

since I was the designated song leader, I introduced choruses. The battle of traditional vs. contemporary began to heat up in this little church. Here I was preaching pretty dry sermons on the "church" and changing things up. This did not bode well for a small conservative Baptist church out in the far North Country.

When we had come to this town, my wife had been told that this was the golden goose church of the conference. Carolyn was from the biggest church in Manitoba and had stints of being their head pianist. They told us if you couldn't make it there, you couldn't make it anywhere. No pressure! The kicker was that she was a perfectionist and had to have everything just right. So I heard this conversation often. It didn't take too long to discover my Ben Franklin list of pro and cons for marrying this girl did not match up with the reality I was experiencing. We were exactly polar opposites in every way. We made twelve thousand a year before taxes, and she managed to save three thousand. She could squeeze a penny out of a penny.

I also thought that since I was married everything would be solved in the bedroom, and perhaps ninety nine percent of the time that's true. I got the one percent and ended up marrying someone who had been taught that sex was dirty and that you 'let him do what he wants to do', but you don't have to enjoy it. Needless to say, I can count the number of times on one hand that we had sex in our two year marriage. Here I had held myself out for seven years by not even kissing another girl to end up with this. This threw a real monkey wrench in things not to mention it messed up my plans. I had dreamed about telling the people of my congregation that you should wait until you're married and that it was the best thing.

The Angel and the Vision

I wanted to tell the young people that it was worth waiting and important to do so. This was the one thing I had not counted on. By the way, who do you talk to about this? I literally had no one to turn to or to confide in about this dilemma. I could not talk to my parents, her parents or anyone else in the church. Here we were, so young in the ministry without any mentors. This was a huge mistake on my part for not starting out as an assistant and being mentored by a senior pastor.

As we neared the end of the first year Carolyn started regressing into a nervous breakdown. The pressures of being a pastor's wife; living in a fish bowl in a small town vs. the big city she was used to; the unyielding pressure of my mom trying to manipulate and dominate and control things across the miles was too much. She started shaking and couldn't stop. Her perception of what it would be like being a Pastor's wife, was not the Cinderella experience that she imagined and living in a fish bowl was becoming too painful. Neither one of us knew how to take the academics of Bible school and translate it into a personal intimate relationship with God or a working relationship with others.

Just a year ago, she would curl up on her Mother's lap. She was the youngest child born more than a dozen years from her nearest sibling. She was extremely pampered by her parents and siblings. That should have been a warning sign. She was longing to go back to that. She missed the quietness and the solitude. She began to think that if she could just get away from me and the church then everything would go back to normal and she would be alright.

The Beginning

One day my mother called to rehearse the evils of not following God wholeheartedly. God's judgment was for those who didn't obey. His judgment was especially for those who didn't listen to what Mother said, thought or believed. I was becoming more and more agitated and frustrated. I just couldn't take it anymore. I just couldn't get far enough away from her. I remember setting the phone down and walking away. Thirty minutes later when I came back, she was still talking. My hands were sweaty and I was shaking like Don Knox. Whenever I talked to my mom, my whole personality would change. I would get very anxious, fearful, angry and moody. I finally came back to pick up the phone and she had hung up. I would usually be moody and agitated for days after that. This time was no different. This had a very adverse effect on our marriage.

Carolyn and I started arguing more. We argued over finances and she began to become more and more suspicious. All the things my mom told her about me were becoming a self fulfilling prophecy. I started regressing back into past sinful behavior of fantasizing. The more I heard the words of death spoken over me, first by my Mom and now my wife, I began to believe that lie rather than the work that God had done in me during Bible School. We slowly became more and more distant. One day she made the comment that she would never have kids with me. That really hurt and only intensified the issues and we continued to grow further and further apart. We were scheduled to go to her parent's house for Christmas. Carolyn took a bus home early. When I got there a week later, she had become completely cold towards me. This would be our last Christmas together because she never came back.

The Angel and the Vision

I came back after Christmas more renewed, and changed my whole sermons. In fact, I began to seek the Lords face more. Those three months became the best time ever for both the congregation and myself, but she would believe none of it.

I finally received enough pressure from the deacons to call and get her back. I was forced to put my foot down and say, "You must come back." They were becoming embarrassed and were afraid what the town would think. This would prove to be premature. I was not prepared for her response. She snapped and said defiantly, "I'm not coming back." She had never been like that before, but the break down had taken its toll. After telling the church that she refused to come back the deacons asked me to resign. They were kind enough to let me stay in the parsonage for three months until I could find a job and get back on my feet.

I waited one year for her to come back and during that time every letter I sent to her was returned unopened. Her Mom and dad stepped in and blamed me for her breakdown. They refused to let me come back and be with her, and rejected all phone calls and letters. They blamed me for everything.

During that time, I took a sales job in the province of Saskatchewan and did extremely well. Despite doing well, I was totally devastated. I had put all my hopes and dreams into being a Pastor and marrying this girl and both were gone. When I finally realized we were never getting back together and that I would never Pastor again, I broke down in a deep despair. I saw no way out. Carolyn's mom told me to never call again and that I would never see her anymore. I was literally beside myself. I felt trapped and cornered. I was in a maze and had hit

The Beginning

a dead end with no bread crumb trail to find a new beginning or a way out. From how I was taught, I could never remarry and I could never Pastor. That was the Davidson and Baptist way. My life, my hopes and dreams were all finished.

I remember the fateful night very clearly. It was the one year anniversary of her going home and never coming back. It was a cold bitter night in that second week of December 1986. I had been in deep despair. I had tried so hard and remained faithful. I had worked so hard that year. I had put up with ridicule for being a Christian from my co workers. I was going to church. Yes, I was trying, but I had just gotten the final blow today. It really was over with my wife. I could never Pastor again and I had spent five years studying. I'd lost my marriage and my career. I had nowhere to turn and no one to turn to. I was disillusioned with myself and God. I looked up into the heavens and said, "I can't do this anymore," I cried out in anguish to God. "I can't live by myself. I'm not wired that way.

The only option I saw was that it was either going to be God or it was going to be women. I honestly did not see any other choice. My soul was in deep anguish as I walked the streets of Regina, Saskatchewan. I could not get a divorce and find some nice person. That was not allowed. I could never remarry and be a Pastor again. That was not allowed. What was there for me to live for? I was stuck with my parents and the Baptist code. It was all or nothing.

Why the dramatic choice between God and women? The reason was because I could not see myself living alone. I felt I had to have someone in my life who loved me. For twenty

The Angel and the Vision

three years, I had performed for God but never had learned or experienced His love.

As I stood there with bitterness and anger surging like a tsunami towards the shore in my heart, I felt trapped and betrayed. I felt nothing but hatred towards my wife, her family, and my parents and more importantly...God. What right did they have to destroy everything I had worked so hard for? I did everything that was asked and everything that was expected. I had done my duty and I had followed all the rules. What had it gotten me but pain? I might as well live for myself. No one else cared for me or loved me. I was all alone.

As the wave gathered momentum and began to reach shore, the hatred began to rise up like a humungous wall as it reached the shore. I remember as I raised my fist towards heaven as I cried out, "Why did you do this to me? Serving you is not worth it." The shoreline was fast receding as a hundred foot wall of hate, anger, unforgiveness and bitterness reached its pinnacle of fury. I paced the streets finding myself totally conflicted as hate filed my heart towards God. After an extended time, I made my choice and I made it out loud. "I choose women, I want nothing more to do with you God" I cried out in anguish. I felt that the tsunami would fill that void in my life, so off I went looking. I had no idea how devastating the results would be.

Up until now I had found my comforts first in fantasizing, then getting several degrees, getting married and finally being a Pastor over a church. None of them had filled the void in my heart. So, now I would pursue the one thing I thought would really satisfy. It was something I had suppressed for the last seven years. This must be the answer. I had made my choice

The Beginning

and left God behind. It should be a no brainer now without the guilt.

I did not find the transition easy, however. I was about to find out the hard way, that whatever I had experienced living in a performance mode in the 'Christian world' was nothing to what I was going to experience in the 'world'. My choice literally lowered me into a deeper level of hell. I had not counted on the demoralizing effects of the tsunami. Now I may not have had a deep relationship with God, but I did have discipline and a structure in my life. I was filled with the Word and character. Now I was about to throw even that away out of my despair. I was about to make total destruction of my heart.

Mom always said that if I started to drink I would become an alcoholic. I think that was one of her ways of trying to scare us kids into not drinking. They really hated drinking because my dad got into so much trouble in his youth. Well part of the pursuit of women involves drinking, smoking and drugs. I had already tried smoking in my youth when I was rebellious and personally hated the smell. My need to be in control brought me to the conclusion that it was a worthless endeavor. So although I turned my back on God for those three years, smoking and drugs was never even a thought in my mind.

> *It only takes one road to lead you to destruction*

I really don't think the devil even cares whether one does all the addictions. He just wanted my heart and my time. He only really needs one or two hooks into you to hold you and bind you. Like the tsunami in the natural setting, the area affected is

The Angel and the Vision

destroyed by water. In other parts of a country it can be by a raging forest fire, or a destructive tornado, or in another an earthquake. Devastation is devastation and any one of the four elements out of control can cause it.

So it is in the spiritual arena. The sexual arena is so vast and multifaceted that between your own desires and the devil binding you into addictions by creating strongholds, your whole world can be swallowed up. It only takes one road to lead you to destruction.

I remember a time when I came out of a bar and I had indulged in too much drink. I really liked the sweet mixed drinks. They went down smooth but were a kicker in the end if you were not careful. I was walking by myself and this guy had two gorgeous girls, one on each arm. He looked at me and laughed out loud as he said, "Looks like you're going home by yourself tonight." He continued to laugh at me as he left with his two beautiful blondes. I was not impressed and the fact that I felt a little tipsy didn't help. This did not stop me in my pursuit of women, but ironically, I resolved never to over drink again. I did not like the feeling of not being in control.

Time passed and I finally started making some hook-ups. If you pursue something long enough you will find it. An interesting note in all this was that I was going after what I thought would fill the emptiness, something that would fill the aching void in my life. I had taken a huge gamble in cursing God. I had totally turned my back on the Lord and was deliberately following after sin. I had forsaken Him, but He never forsook me. I was having sex with these women who were trying to fill their emptiness and verses would go through my mind.

The Beginning

I see now that He was always there. His presence and his angels watched and kept guard. I was eternally loved and valued. God saw in me what I did not see in myself, and He was the loving Father standing at the door longing for the time when I would be sick of filling myself with the empty husks from the pig trough. Many times after I had left a girl's house, I would shake my head and be mumbling to myself, "What am I doing, it feels like I am eating corn stalks." It was a hollow filling. The insides of my chest felt like I had taken a blow torch and torched the walls of my heart.

So back I went, getting more and more miserable. I found each girl produced more disappointment. They were acting as shallow as I and were filled with deep selfishness. It finally got to the point, several years in, where I was just plain sick of it, and then I met Clare.

By now I was dating three girls at one time and had vowed I would never marry. I was deeply bitter and selfish, but a mutual friend of ours was convinced that we were the right couple. She obviously saw in me what I could not see in myself. Clare thought I was disgusting and wanted nothing to do with me.

Clare was a pure innocent soul. She had never had a boyfriend and came from a solid loving Catholic family. She was innocent. Her whole life revolved around working hard enough to put her siblings through school. She was deeply family oriented and had already devoted the last nine years of her life by sending all her extra money back home to her native country the Philippines to give them a chance to have a better life than they had grown up having. They had grown up in a small bamboo hut in a small village and were extremely poor. At

The Angel and the Vision

sixteen years of age she got a job in Spain working for a rich actor and automobile manufacturer owner. She wanted her family to have a better life than she had and was willing to do whatever she could to change that. She had spent the last nine years there being a nanny for his kids and had just moved to Toronto, Canada in the last six months.

Getting married to Clare probably saved my life. I put my partying ways behind me, but I did not totally devote myself to the Lord. This being said, one needs something to fill that void and I found it next in possessions and trying to get rich. I tried to shortcut my way to success and tried several quick rich schemes to get there. I went back to being religious and had added a new comfort in gaining money and possessions. Clare usually cried herself to sleep while I indulged myself in self destructive ways that ended up in more bad judgment and financial ruin.

I kept looking for things to fill me up whether it was expensive clothes, riches, business success or perfect credit. None of it satisfied and with each failure, I became more disillusioned and angry. Numerous business failures, bankruptcies and poor investments drove me into deeper and deeper despair.

Why Clare agreed to marry me is still somewhat a mystery to both of us. I sensed deep in my soul that she was the right person for me. I did write her parents asking for her hand and blessing in marriage and that really made a deep impact on them. One of the things that go to the character of Clare was a question she asked herself before we got married. "Could she accept the whole package the way it was?" In other words

The Beginning

could she love me and learn to love me without trying to change me. So she did just that and placed me in God's hand and made the choice to love me the way I was.., both the good and bad. She still cried herself to sleep every night.

A crack in the wall of my ego happened in late 1999 when several events transpired in my life. Everything that I was putting my trust in was crumbling. I was heading into my second financial meltdown. We had a great concept in home improvement and had built the business up to six salesmen and 30 crews. Unfortunately, we grew too fast without a solid business plan or proper accounting. We miscalculated the cost of running the business and we got into areas that cost us greatly. My greatest mistake was letting a guy set up the whole structure for the sales crew and the costs and products we marketed without a good accountant backing us up. This was someone that my wife did not approve of either. She thought I should stay small and continue being my own sales force while directing the company. At the time we met this guy we were doing well and was profitable with three to four crews. We would end up becoming bankrupt both personally and in business by letting this guy into our life.

I remember the day the tow truck came and hauled away our work trailer and my wife's Jeep Cherokee. I sat in the living room livid and filled with rage. I crashed my hand down on the marble table and literally broke it in half. My wife had made an innocent comment to me that I took personally. I began screaming out of control. I told her we were finished; I went upstairs to get the remaining money we had left and said that I was leaving.

The Angel and the Vision

I went down the street to the nearest motel and stayed there for three days and nights hugging my box of money. I eventually felt so stupid and was by now realizing how much I missed my wife and kids. I ran into them at the local grocery store and we ended up talking. This is the beauty of my wife. She thought it was more comical than serious. She gracefully defused the situation and we began talking things through. A new direction had to be made. We were just butting our heads over and over into a brick wall.

Up until this point I was skating spiritually. I was the last one in church on Sunday and the first one out. We attended a large mega church that allowed us to kind of melt into the scenery. But that was about to change.

We started over in a new construction business. This time I did it smarter. We eventually got involved in a small little church. Within a couple years I was doing very well in that construction business, but I was also becoming hungrier for God.

It was now 2005 and God was bringing me to a point of total devotion to Himself. Or should I say that God was always arranging things to bring me to a point of total devotion to him, the difference now was that He had both my ears. One night at a prayer meeting I said, "Whatever it takes." This was not a flippant prayer, but something that had been stirring deeply within me for some time. There had been a challenge by one of the Prophetic voices in our church who questioned me. She said rather bluntly, "Are you sure?" I hesitated slightly as certain events flashed before my face, and then without further hesitation said, "Yes!" The adventure had begun.

The Beginning

It was several months later that one of the elders in our church gave a message and shared how Theophostic ministry had changed his life and that he was opening up ministry to all who wanted it. I was so hungry and desperate for God and after hearing his testimony I felt deeply stirred inside. I found myself still reacting certain ways and not knowing why. Most of the 'comfort' things in my life were still there in some form or another. I was holding on to these 'comforts' to fill the deep void I had inside.

Not truly understanding the ramifications or impact of that choice, I was willing for God to come into my life to do whatever He chose to do so that the freedom of God would be released in my life. A choice was made to be one of those people. By "those", I meant someone who was desperate to know God and do whatever it took to see that happen.

I was tired of being apathetic for the last twenty years and wanted more. Why was I making the same mistakes over and over? I wanted answers and I wanted freedom. The effects of the spiritual tsunami were still there. I needed help getting things cleaned up and rebuilt. This commitment to that elder continued regularly for three years. We would get together more than fifty times for two hour sessions. I began to ask Jesus to come in and reveal areas where there were painful memories or wounds that needed to be healed. We would then ask Jesus to come in and bring healing and cleansing in those areas.

> *I was willing for God to come into my life to do whatever he chose to do so that the freedom of God would be released in my life.*

The Angel and the Vision

The most awesome time of my life began to reveal itself over the next twelve months. As I let God come in, He spoke to the secret places of my heart and healing took place. Aspects of God's character began to be opened up to me in a supernatural revelation. God revealed who He was in wonderful pictures by giving a revelation of the grace of God and the mercy of God in living color.

For the next twelve months all that I could see was the love of God. Jesus came into those past memories, one by one, where there had been great pain and belief systems formed out of that pain. These were wrong belief systems that had triggered fear, worry, guilt and anger.

Up until this point, I had been having a hard time understanding how this hunger for God, which was so great, would be present, and then something would trigger within me and I would be like a wild hair going in a different direction. Tears of repentance and sorrow would follow this and the pattern would repeat itself.

My hardened heart became soft and tears flowed freely. The Lord could hardly be talked about without crying. His love was so real.

One day in January 2006, our pastor put out the challenge to give up the most important thing in our lives for forty days and spend that time pursuing a relationship with God. I immediately said 'yes' and then backed up to consider what cost I had just relinquished. My greatest love was professional basketball and my team was surging towards the finals in first place. Over nine hours a week of my "first love" would have to be given up to spend time with God. After pausing for a

The Beginning

moment and counting the cost, the answer was "Ok, let's do it" and the adventure began.

Within two weeks, God's voice was clearer than ever before. His presence in my life was going to new depths and a hunger and thirst was growing like leaps and bounds. It was as if someone had put salt in my oats, and I wanted more of the living water.

Around the third week an explosion began as I pursued God's presence and I found spontaneous songs coming forth. These songs cried out for more of God. They were new songs birthed from deep within my spirit. They flowed from the well of His presence and I penned my first song in more than twenty years. That song would become the title song of a worship album that I would release a year and a half later.

Ironically, or maybe not so ironic, the title song was 'More of You'. Amazing things were happening while writing these songs down. One of the songs came in a vision where a stone was seen in an underwater cave in the River of Life. This song came alive with music that you could literally see. As the stone was picked up, light came out of the stone and a song could not only be heard, but the notes and melodies came out of the stone in a three dimensional way. It was super awesome! Every sense was heightened. You could taste, feel, hear, touch and see the song.

There was a sweetness and beauty that was hard to imagine or describe and yet everything seemed so beautiful. More important was the fact that I could taste, smell, see, hear and touch the Lord in a very real way. After awakening from this vision in my living room, I wrote down the words as fast as humanly possible. The title song ended up becoming a favorite.

The Angel and the Vision

That song was titled "Deep in Your Presence." By the end of that year, twenty five songs of love and worship to the Lord had been written. God's love, grace and mercy were now flowing in music through the depths of my spirit. Healing was happening in an amazing way.

One of the books that were very helpful to me during this time besides living in the Psalms was a book by Dr. Dale Fife called *The Secret Place*. This book helped paint a picture of passionately pursing the presence of God and gave me the courage to write this book. It was my own beginning to seeing God.

Despite all this, something still seemed to be missing. It was hard to put it all together. There was growth, there was writing of music and still pursuing God, yet life still seemed more like a stock market graph than the flight of an airplane. There was a desire for more consistent highs. I was dissatisfied and wanted more. Just telling God "whatever it takes" was not enough. There had to be an absolute devotion to whatever it takes.

Up to this point, there seemed to be the approach of working towards something rather than "it is finished." There seemed to be a calling Jesus 'Lord' with conditions. There was not calling Him Lord, 'it is finished'.

It was at this time that this vision was manifested. It was during a time of longing for more of the Lord at whatever the cost. No longer did I want to be an average Christian or a normal Christian; I wanted to be that one man that God was searching for as He roamed the earth to fill the gap. A freedom of abandonment was felt within me to be a radical Christian. To experience everything God was willing to impart within a

The Beginning

desperate life that did not care what the cost was. But it had to be for the right reason. And you know what, He heard that inner cry.

This vision did not come all at once. The majority of it actually stretched over about a three month period. The vision came at different times of the day and night. Sometimes I would sit at the computer and just see it. Typing could not happen fast enough. Not wanting to be influenced by similar books or themes, I pretty much just read my Bible. If God had something to say to me, let Him speak. Sometimes it manifested itself while driving or during quiet times; very often it was during the late night or early morning. I tried to stay true to hear what I was seeing and referenced only the Bible to ascertain or confirm its accuracy. I tried not to help the characters along with my personal agenda.

Being a writer or pursing such an idea had never been a passion. However, grace and purpose were strongly present. When this vision came, I saw and I wrote. What I saw was intensely real as if I was there, and I saw everything in vivid color and detail.

I would learn layering. What I mean by that is that the Lord taught me to often go back to the same vision and learn the ability to look around within that vision. I ended up coming back to some areas of the vision several times and was able to see more of what happened in that area or things that I missed the first time.

Everything that was revealed in this vision was first seen as applying to me. The vision of my perception of the church and every aspect of it, I saw first in me. If I didn't see it, the Lord

The Angel and the Vision

was pretty quick to reveal it to me. That which was seen was quickly repented of. I came to realize that there are many things in my life I do not see clearly, but that are so evident to others. God is an expert in revealing the things within, that one tries to hide even from oneself.

There might be some who don't see such a stringent need for repentance and think that everything is OK both with them and with the church; that would, of course, be me for the first forty five years of my life.

It is easy to disregard truth, harden your hearts, and become confused and double minded. That struggle is easy to understand. The tendency is to live in "absolutely I will not surrender". I will choose as to when, where and how much.

> *I would have to experience repentance before I would be able to live in real relationship,*

The important thing is that I would have to experience repentance before I would be able to live in real relationship. Even going through the valley of the shadow of death to experience my road to repentance, though, He was right there beside me.

It is said that God speaks to us in a still small voice, His Word and through his people. When we do not listen, then He speaks to us in dreams and visions. When that doesn't work we find ourselves being embattled with sickness and disease, and wonder how the devil was able to establish a foothold in our life.

It is so easy to call something God's will when in reality it is reaping what we have sown. The reality is that we choose

The Beginning

rebellious ideas and prideful ambitions and actually step out of relationship with God. That would be me. It was my choice.

Being left vulnerable, one gets eaten alive by the world system they embrace; a devil bent on destroying them and their own flesh that is prone to serve itself. One quickly forget that one does not fight against flesh and blood, but it is a spiritual battle with real enemies, and those principalities and powers that one cannot see with their natural eyes, see them very well and looks for any opening to trip them up.

It is amazing how our disobedience and bent to holding on to our sin drags and sucks us into a quicksand of death. We become "spiritually" proud that we are not like that other person over 'there' that is a sinner. We thank God we are not like Him. We forget that what we should do is fall on our faces and ask God to be merciful to us. None of us stand perfect before God in our own righteousness. It is His righteousness in us.

We must be willing to cut off the thing that offends us and drags us down. For me, it was TV and Internet. It was in getting rid of those two things and choosing to devote myself to God's Word and seeking His presence that opened me up to this precious vision which is God's gift to the body of Christ. There had to be a putting away of those things for a season so that my eyes could be open and my ears could hear His voice.

I pray that you can easily identify with my story and be able to experience a new revelation of freedom and life in your relationship with the Lord. We all have this common thread of struggling to learn that Jesus is more than enough. Of learning that we can fully and completely trust the Lord and believe His

The Angel and the Vision

Word that it is relevant and completely true for our life. Of knowing that we are totally valued and that our life does make a difference to God. We are not abandoned and we are not rejected.

Join me as Christ opens the clay vessel with the rod of His scepter so that His unsurpassable and amazing fragrance will be released to a world that is frantic for a new essence.

Well, this clay vessel was about to be messed with big time. I had said in complete desperation "Whatever it takes." This is what can happen when you say that and really mean it.

The Beginning

Notes

2

THE ANGEL AND THE VISION

It was a bright sunny day In Michigan. I had felt a desire to get alone in quiet solitude with God and spend an extended time in worship. I decided to stop by my church and play piano and just worship and praise the king.

For about a month now, I had been working on a new song called, "*I long for You Lord,*" My passion for Him was growing daily, and my intimacy with Him was growing stronger and stronger. What a delight to be in His presence praising and worshipping the Lord God of the Universe. This new song expressed how much I longed for the Lord. He is a consuming fire and relationship with Him meant cleaning out the misconceptions of the old self and its desires, and letting God's love flow through me. I wanted the longing to increase and anything that came between the Lord and me had to be cleansed out and renewal to come in.

The Angel and the Vision

I prayed quietly yet fervently to the Lord, "Change my thinking and increase my faith." Little did I know that within a couple months, this song would be the red carpet that would be the blueprint to getting me out of the maze I found myself in.

As I played this song of longing which God had birthed within me, I continued to praise and honor the Lord of Lords. I'm not sure how long I had been singing when I felt a distinct presence in the church sanctuary. I felt the hair creep up on the back of my neck and felt a distinct change in the atmosphere. I looked back thinking someone had walked in. I was astounded to see as clearly as I would see anyone, an angel standing at the back of the church. I had a sense that I had been caught up in the spirit and was able to see clearly into the spirit realm. He was absolutely huge as he straddled the double doors at the back of the church.

He stood there with both legs spread on either sides of the double doors. He stood about eighteen to twenty plus feet tall. You could see the doors between His legs as he was wearing what looked to be like a tunic that came down to his knees. The bottom of his tunic was at the top of the door.

The material looked to be of a bright white linen material with a brownish material accenting the short sleeves and hem of his tunic. A simple belt completed his dress. Immediately, you were drawn to his eyes for they were pools of dark turquoise filled with wisdom and strength. His hair was a short blond cut that gave a look of determination and purpose. His very presence commanded your attention. In his hand he held a large sword; similar to what you might have seen in a Roman movie or middle-aged movie of conquering knights.

The Angel and the Vision

The sword was very unique in that it was completely immersed in a blue fire that radiated from the blade. It was a very definite, ominous picture of strength. He appeared to be an angel of warfare and yet he had no armor on him other than his sword.

I stared at the glistening sword as it was being waved back and forth, side-to-side, from his left to his right. He was repeatedly saying three words, "**Form, Fullness, and Fruitfulness**".

I fell to my knees in great trepidation knowing I was in the presence of God. It was obvious to me that this was not a social call. A spirit of purposefulness and holiness had settled on the room like the morning dew.

As I lay bent over on my knees with head bowed, the angel said to me, "Get up and do not be afraid for I have been sent by the Master, the living Lord and Savior Jesus Christ to show you the things that are to come. These are things that greatly affect your life and those around you."

"The Master has heard the prayers of a few of His saints and your hearts desire, and I have been commissioned to give a message to you and God's people." I arose from my knees and sat back down on the piano bench.

"What have the saints been praying?" I asked quietly. I was curious to know what would bring such a grand spectacle to my door.

"The Master has heard the cries of those who travail for the souls of men, those who are caught up in apathy and sin and don't see the end result of their futility. He has heard the

The Angel and the Vision

prayers of those who seek to go to a deeper level of fruitfulness."

The angel stopped speaking to me and went back to saying, "form, fullness, and fruitfulness", over and over again. Finally, he stopped and looking me straight in the eye saying, "This message is for the whole church, not just for you. I am here to show you the devastation of what is going on in the heavenlies in the church. There is a warfare going on for the hearts of men and this church has grown stagnant."

"The church is stagnant," I thought in bewilderment. I thought the church was at least cruising; at least that is how our church seemed to be.

"What you see with your natural sight is most often the opposite in the spirit realm", the angel said to me.

I pondered these words of wisdom. "God's ways are neither our ways nor his thoughts our thoughts," I mused.

PART I

FORM OF GODLINESS

The Angel and the Vision

The angel elaborated on the words he was commissioned to give. "The master has looked and weighed the hearts of his people and had found them to be wanting. He has found his people to be living in a form- **a form of godliness**."

"This was not sounding good. The sternness of the angel's voice along with the fire in His eyes caused my heart to pound greatly.

Where had I heard this 'form of godliness' from? I racked my mind as I tried to steady myself. From a child I had memorized thousands of verses and searched my brain frantically to remember where I had seen this phrase. I finally had to pull my concordance out to find out where these words were spoken of in the Word of God for I had a foreboding impression that the context of that proclamation would explain the context of the angel's words. I found 'form of godliness' in 2 Timothy 3, and began reading anxiously:

> "But mark this. There will be terrible times in the last days. People will be lovers of themselves, lovers of money, boastful, proud, abusive, disobedient to their parents, ungrateful, unholy,
>
> Without love, unforgiving, slanderous, without self control, brutal, not lovers of the good, treacherous, rash, conceited, lovers of pleasure rather than lovers of God---<u>having a form of godliness but denying its power</u>."
>
> (2 Timoth3:1-5) NIV

My heart beat in strong measured staccato as I pondered wildly the last part, which said, "Having a form of godliness but

The Angel and the Vision

denying its power." The words "denying its power" jumped off the pages and a clue began to formulate slowly within me.

"There is something that is very significant here," I reasoned intuitively while pondering this bold statement.

The angel replied soberly, "God's people are denying His power. They have denied a power of Godliness and are living in abject unbelief. They love what they can see and touch with their eyes; things they can touch and taste and grab hold of but they are living their life out by what pleases them. They do not believe the promises of God. They have let the things of this world come in and choke out the Word. They do not understand God's forgiveness and are filled with bitterness and hatred towards those around them. This has been the cause of much sickness and disease.

God has not given his people a spirit of fear but of love, power and a sound mind. So many have become lost and do not know how to experience God's love."

I remembered it saying in 1 John 2:14: KJV

> *"Love not the World neither the things that are in the World, if any man loves the World the love of the father is not in him."*

I reasoned within myself that if God's love, power and a sound mind are something to be received, and I am not turning towards God completely but am receiving other substitutes into my life and heart; then it is possible that I could be living out of a shell of religion. It would become a pure knowledge of formulas, lingos and mere talk but without really being totally

The Angel and the Vision

committed to a relationship of intimacy with God. If this is really true, does this mean I am merely fooling myself?

The angel interrupted my deep thoughts by responding passionately, "God's people do not believe God's promises. They do not believe what God's Word says; they are not acting in faith. Faith comes by hearing and hearing by the word of God and God's people are not in His Word. They read it but do not hear it. They come and worship God on Sunday and then they forget about Him the rest of the week. They are missing the mark. They are living in sin."

As I stood face to face with the angel, my legs shook violently as a sense of conviction began to come over my own soul. The blood drained from my face and I began to feel queasy in my stomach.

I said fervently, almost under my breath, "I am guilty of that." I didn't know about anyone else in our church, but I saw three or four thing's for sure that applied to me here. Everything about these verses indicated self-absorption to the exclusion of others. Slowly, I began to mentally count the things that pertained to me. I found myself being a lover of myself. I seemed to take care of myself very well. What I wanted came first. I was the king of my castle and things had better be done right. I was currently paying a huge price for my love of money. Bad business decisions had effectively wiped out the nest egg that I had built and my net worth had dropped to one third of its original. It also seemed I was having a harder and harder time forgiving people.

The hardest thing for me was having very little self-control. I had ballooned up to three hundred and twenty five pounds, and had gained thirty five pounds in the last year and a half alone.

The Angel and the Vision

The sad part is that I didn't feel a confidence as to how to stop it or even turn it around. I was also watching up to forty hours of TV a week, not to mention countless hours on the Internet trying various businesses. My thought life seemed double minded and I had a hard time controlling my thoughts. Yet, I was busy in church. I was part of the worship team and taught a men's group.

Despite my involvement and apparent zeal, I felt sluggish with little energy and my body ached all the time. God had done so much in my life these last three years since I had cried out to Him in desperation, "Whatever it takes". But my life still felt like the stock market, having its highs and its lows. I was longing for more consistent highs. I found myself still saying words like, "I can't help myself" or "I can't believe I did that again." Was this the way it should be?

> *It is not just some words on paper but the resounding revelatory proceeding Word of God.*

The angel spoke with a deep resonance that shook me to my core. "The church has become comfortable. God's people are to live by faith and not by sight. If you live by sight you are not walking by faith. God's people know all about Him. They can talk very easily about Him, yet they put Him aside when it is convenient for them."

My mind came back to the reality of the moment as the angel related words that he had been commissioned to give me from the Master.

The Master says that His people have denied His power; a power that comes from living in His love. They honor Him with their lips, but their hearts are far from me. The things of this

The Angel and the Vision

world have choked out the Word in their lives. They have decided for themselves what is right and wrong.

"If people only realized how critical and essential the Word is in the life of a believer," I thought to myself.

Again, I pondered those words in 1 John 2:14 KJV that said,

> *"Love not the world, neither the things that are in the World, if anyone loves the World the love of the Father is not in them."*

Having a form of godliness in our life surely meant that a person was "worldly" and that God's love was not present in their life. Without a deep love and relationship with the Lord, a form of godliness was sure to find its way into my heart and life.

I began to shudder as the implication of being double minded was revealed for the raw force of evil that it was. Truly, it was an excellent tool of the enemy to allow us to entertain a form of godliness so we could feel good about ourselves, and that at least we are making an attempt to have God in our life. One might even be talking about God all the time and yet, in his life, actions, and his heart it was all about himself.

I found myself beginning to justify to myself that although I struggled with sin in my life, I was trying to give God some time during the week. Sure it was a token of my devotion, but I was trying. Was that not good enough?

The angel began to discourse with me about how man could only reach God through faith. How nothing could please God except faith and obedience. It was about the kind of faith and obedience that knows God intimately and without doubting. Everything must be done in faith and undergirded by love. I

The Angel and the Vision

was beginning to see that I really did not understand the Word of God. I was barely reading it, so how could I understand the power of God's love and Word to change my life. I was depending on the pastor's messages and music to sustain me. I was reading every other book, but God's Word. I did not understand its critical importance—that it is not just some words on paper, but the resounding revelatory proceeding Word of God

The angel explained how the Word of God must vibrate within me. There must be such a sense of fullness of the Word that it is on my lips and ready to use at a moment's notice. It should be alive and fun. This kind of understanding and knowledge comes from meditating and chewing on His promises day and night.

> *I began to shudder as the implication of being double minded was revealed for the raw force of evil that it was*

"It is alive and able to change about the worst possible situation," the angel said fervently. "When Jesus died on the cross He proclaimed boldly, 'it is finished'. People do not understand the absolute power, finality, and importance of that statement. When Jesus Christ sat down at the right hand of the throne of God, he gave His redeemed the same authority and power He had on this earth. He gave His people full access to the throne room of God."

As the words of the angel registered in my conscious mind, I was reminded of a message I had just been listening to from Thurman Scrivener, a Pastor from the Living Savior Ministries in Texas, regarding how God's promises were like a safety deposit box. In the earthly sense the banker has one key and you have

The Angel and the Vision

one key. He puts his key in and you put yours in, and you can get access to its contents. Well, in the spiritual realm, Jesus has already put His key in, turned it and sat down at the right hand of the throne of God. He has declared it to be finished.

We weakly ask God to do things for us, and yet He is saying it is already finished. He has already turned his key and given our key to us. These keys are in the Word; we have to find them and learn how to use them. These keys have everything to do with our faith and believing God's promises without doubting. I would remember this later and it would have a much greater significance.

The angel explained ardently that God's Word is forever settled in heaven, but must be exercised on earth through our faith without any doubt in our heart. The only way to please the Master is to diligently seek him... Our reward comes when we diligently seek him. It is to be a living faith that comes through relationship. I pondered this thought of diligence. I remembered Hebrews 11:6 KJV saying,

> *It is to be a living faith that comes through relationship with God*

> "But without faith it is impossible to please God, because anyone who comes to God must believe that He exists and that He is a rewarder of those who diligently seek Him."

"How do you get that faith?" I pondered. I thought that if we are being convicted of a form of godliness, which is also a spirit of religion, then it couldn't be something we could do to receive the glory and credit for. Otherwise we are doing it in our strength, which are a form of godliness and a spirit of religion.

The Angel and the Vision

Wow, my head was certainly spinning as I thought of the complexity! It is so easy to fall into this religious spirit. I found this was quickly driving me to my knees. I must seek God's face and voice lest I fall into deception and error. I found myself repeating this over and over, "Is not faith something you do, and wouldn't that be something I could easily take credit for?" It was a valid statement and I would wrestle with this for a long time before I found the answer.

The angel continued on by saying, "Faith comes by hearing and hearing by the Word of God. God's people are dying of a myriad of diseases and sicknesses because they have not hidden God's Word in their heart; they do not pursue passionately to know and understand God's will and ways for their life. They live hollow and empty because they keep filling themselves with the wrong things. You need to hear the Word of God through a revelation of the spirit. If you do not meditate on God's word day and night, then you will open yourself up to the enemy. You will die rather than live that which is your purpose and destiny. God's people are substituting everything else for their perception of life and are not making His Word the primary source."

I considered the angels words carefully. God's will is that we worship and serve Him in Spirit and in truth. It is to be a living faith that comes through relationship. Faith is not faith in our faith, but believing without doubting in God's promises. It is knowing God's Word so well and spending so much time in intimate relationship with Him that there is just no doubt in your heart. I felt like I understood this somewhat in my head but that most of what the angel said was flying right past me. I needed to hear more. I needed revelation to pierce through the fog of my thinking

3

THE FOG

The angel interrupted my musings and said with deep urgency, "Come with me. I have something to show you." We proceeded to walk around the church auditorium in a slow measured gait for several minutes.

"I am going to reveal what is happening in the Spirit. You must give your complete attention and focus to what I am about to show you." Reaching forth his hand, the angel held out a small container, "Before I do that, take these things and put them in your eyes."

"What are they?" I replied mystified as I reached for the canister. I popped open the top with a low grunt and saw two lenses within a milky substance.

"Those are special contact lenses. This is a set of lens within a set of lenses. They are special and only for you. Here hold it up to the light and I will show you." I held one of the lenses between my forefinger and thumb and extended it up to the

The Angel and the Vision

light. As I peered at it in the light I observed what looked like round bubbles swirling within the lens itself.

"What does this mean?" I asked with an puzzled uncertainty, while scrunching my eyebrows together so they almost touched. I strained to look closer at the lenses.

"Those," replied the angel candidly, "are lenses of revelation. These lenses are unique in that they allow you the ability to see things at a different level in the spirit realm."

I squirted some ointment on the lenses that the angel provided and tilted my head back while proceeding to put the contact lenses in. I pressed my eyes open and shut several times as I tried to focus.

"Are they in?" the angel asked, with a question mark and a mild concern in his voice.

"Yeah they are in, but I can't seem to focus," I replied with a slight frustration.

"Humph! That's because I haven't given the word yet," the angel said in a matter of fact tone. "These contacts are a gift from God. They are the *Seer's lens*. For now on I will remotely control the lens, but eventually you will have to learn how to move between the lenses to see things on different levels."

The lens within the lens rotated to their designated position as the angel spoke with a calming ease yet with an obvious authority, and immediately a fog appeared that lay over the whole auditorium.

"Be careful not to get proud because you have these lenses. You will only be able to see in bits and pieces so you must be

The Fog

humble and listen, because not all is to be interpreted as it seems."

I hardly heard what the angel said as I was becoming caught up in this new phenomenon. It would be one of the most important lessons missed as I began this journey.

I blinked several times again as I tried to focus and felt a damp wetness lay like a wet towel against my cheeks. The wetness, I would discover, was this dense, black ominous fog that lay like a thick cloud over the lower part of the sanctuary from about ground level to roughly eight feet up.

Feeling a bit irritable, I inquired of the angel, "I thought you gave the word. It's worse than it was before. What is this? It's all foggy."

"This fog," said the angel bluntly "Represents this 'form of godliness' that I spoke of to you earlier. You are actually seeing quite clearly. When you honor God with your lips, but your heart is far from Him, you have denied His power. It is also this denial that creates this fog."

I pondered this scripture in my heart and wondered how even as I was trying to put God first in my life, I was still missing something crucial here. Could this be what I was missing?

"How do we deny God's power?" I asked knowing I did not even have a clue..

"You do not believe God's promises. You are choosing and picking what makes you feel comfortable," the angel said solemnly. "You are choosing religion without relationship."

The Angel and the Vision

A noise began to manifest itself in my ears like the sound of a thousand tree frogs in the evening and continued to grow louder. Ignoring all this, I brushed right past the relationship part as I tried to think of what kind of promises God would be talking about. I mean, what made me 'comfortable' so to speak? Suddenly several scriptures flooded my mind;

> *"If you abide in me and my words abide in you. You may ask for whatever you wish and it will be given to you."*

(John 15:7) NKJV

> *Have faith in God, Jesus answered, I tell you the truth, if anyone says to this mountain, Go, throw yourself into the sea, and does not doubt in his heart, but believes that what he says will happen, it will be done for him. Therefore I tell you whatever you ask for in prayer, <u>believe that you have received it,</u> and it will be yours."*

(Mark 11:22-24) NIV

> I was to be so obedient to God and His Word that when His Spirit prompted me, I would do whatever He asked me to do because of my love relationship with Him

An apprehension began to well up within me. Suddenly, I felt uncomfortable. The noise in my ears grew louder. I sucked in a deep breath as my heart pounded within my chest. These were the kind of promises that required faith without doubting. They were the kind of promises that you could not claim with your natural mind. I usually brushed over these verses casually while disregarding their meaning. I began to pull on my collar as I began to feel more and more like a cat on a hot tin roof. "Is this for real?" I reasoned within myself. "If the Bible says it, can I

The Fog

believe it at face value?" My heart continued to beat hard within me like a battering ram on an old building being torn down to make room for the new.

Speaking into existence something that does not currently exist, truthfully, terrified me. I was not at ease with this. I was at ease with worshipping God on Sunday, praying here and there, and saying I was a Christian, but this was sounding a little radical. I could study the Bible, worship with my friends, talk about God, but to be personally involved with God on a one-to-one level was at best, terrifying.

I toyed with the thought further as I mused about what I had just heard…I was to become so immersed in the Word that it consumed my time. Wow, this was like new revelation! How was I to do that and still get everything else done?

I tried to clear my mind and ease my beating heart as I took several slow breaths trying to slow down my heart beat. The angel said that I was to get God's Word so in my heart that it radically changed me. I was to be so obedient to God and His Word that when His Spirit prompted me, I would do whatever He asked to do because of my love relationship with Him.

My passion to do things was kicking in, and I began to feel stressed out further as I contemplated all that the angel was telling me. I started asking myself if I was actually willing to look expectantly for opportunities to lay hands on the sick and guarantee them that they were healed because God's Word said so. Doubt and unbelief flooded my heart, and a slow terror began to rise within like a burning in my throat.

"So this is what a form of godliness is," I thought. "I am denying God's power. I am saying that maybe God can heal

The Angel and the Vision

others, but He can't heal through me?" My flesh began to rise up and squirm like it should do something to make this right. I felt frozen; I didn't know what to do. Hmmmm! Something did not feel right here. I did not even realize it, but I had already caught myself in the first trap. I had breezed by the first part of the verse that talked about abiding, and was already focusing on what I should do.

An early childhood verse wafted through my brain like a gentle breeze;

> "But when he asks he must believe and not doubt, because he who doubts is like a wave of the sea blown and tossed by the wind. That man should not think he will receive anything from the Lord, he is a double minded man, unstable in all he does."
>
> (James 1:6) KJV

> I asked myself if I was actually willing to look expectantly for opportunities to lay hands on the sick and guarantee them that they were healed because God's Word said so

I was beginning to understand why I was having a hard time trusting God. My own form of godliness was from not knowing Jesus passionately and personally. I was not having an intimate relationship with Him.

What does this mean though? Even in saying the word 'intimate', it was not something I could see or feel. It seemed rather abstract. What does it mean to 'know' Him? Do I not have relationship with Him? I felt a cold apprehension slither up my spine and settle as a knot in my back. I really felt that everything that was happening to me at this point with the angel was my own attempt to grapple with my intellect to

The Fog

understand what he was saying. I was fast coming to the conclusion that I didn't have a clue.

The angel sensing my apprehension and complete confusion said, "Doubt and unbelief are the source of a form of godliness, and it creates a fog of confusion in the believer. You want to serve God, but on your terms. It will never work. That person will be unstable and double minded, and will never know true fullness in his life. He will be like a fruit tree with no fruit on it. Let me show you what this fog (**form of g**odliness) has done to you and others like yourself."

He waved his hand in a sideways motion as if to brush aside the fog. As he did that, he snapped his fingers. Immediately, I felt the lens rotate clockwise in my eyes and suddenly I was able to see even more clearly inside the fog. I was immediately and completely horrified at what confronted me. Apparently I had just gone to a deeper spiritual level. I jumped back stumbling over someone lying on the ground. I saw a group of disfigured people milling aimlessly around. This group of people had just come into focus, and I was horrified to see that so many of them did not have any eyes or ears. Some had what looked like vice grips clamped on to their tongues. Many were lame or missing a leg, foot or arms. I noticed that several of them had the tendons cut in the backs of their heels, and they were trying to crawl across the ground.

I looked in abject disbelief at what was in front of me and asked the angel, "What is this. Is this the condition of my friends? Is this the church? I don't see many healthy people here and why are so many disfigured?" I sidestepped a man who had a gash in his side and blood was pouring out. "Why are those people vomiting on each other over here?" I coiled

The Angel and the Vision

back in disgust as one person hurled on his 'friend', and then the other hurled and vomited all over his friend and someone else. It looked like a hurling contest; like who could out hurl the other. I wrinkled my nose at the bad smell that seemed to permeate the air and felt the stench causing a gage reflex in my throat.

"This is what happens when you deny God's power. This is what happens when you decide to make up your own set of rules as to what being a Christian is supposed to be. This is what it means to have religion without relationship with God. When you honor God with your lips, but believe with doubt in your heart, you give place to the world, your flesh and the devil. The enemy is looking for whomever he can to deceive and devour. The devil comes to maim, kill, and destroy. He is desperate for your worship. He is desperate for you adoration. Let me show you some more." He again moved his hand in a sideways motion, snapped his fingers, and it was like a whole new level of the spiritual realm was opened even further to me. The lens swirled and changed again.

> Doubt and unbelief are the source of a form of godliness and it creates a fog of unbelief

A new focus came into view and I now saw several people standing by dozens of deformed people; some were helping people dress or undress, some were combing people's hair and giving them back rubs. They were doing everything possible to make them feel comfortable. They seemed to look like doctors, nurses, coaches, drivers, therapists, and every kind of occupation.

The Fog

This is very nice picture, I thought. These people are being ministered to.

"Who are these nice people?" I asked the angel with deep appreciation. I found myself drawn to their apparent selflessness.

"They are not nice people, they are demons!" the angel admonished sharply.

"What!" I exclaimed with great alarm, "What do you mean they are demons?"

"Look closer," the angel said urgently, snapping his fingers. Suddenly, the true identity of these characters was revealed. What a horrendous site! What I thought to be nice people of various occupations ministering to God's people in the church, were actually not people at all.

These henchmen had disguised themselves in peoples' thoughts to be ministering angels of mercy. What at first I saw in the spirit realm to be one thing, was actually another. They were the devil's henchmen!

"Wow, you could easily be deceived!" I thought while shaking my head profusely. They were actually wolves in sheep's clothing.

As I turned to look at the faces of each person, I saw an object in front of them. On closer inspection, it was an object of either wood, stone, plastic or metal. The henchmen had convinced them to worship the object. The henchmen were holding the object on a string and letting it swing in front of their eyes like a pendulum. The people had accepted the items and were fascinated by them. They seemed to be in a trance or

The Angel and the Vision

were hypnotized. All their energies and time became wrapped up in the item. Many people had hats with the item item dangling off the tip of the hat. It had stopped being something the henchmen were dangling and they had received it and welcomed it into their life.

Every henchman seemed to have an assignment. In one corner, a head demon was holding a numeric counter in his hand. He was instructing a group of lesser demons to take something away from the person that they were assigned to. Some of the devil's henchmen were assigned to one person, and others had two, three and up to a dozen or more. Some henchmen were even reaching inside of bodies and were giving headaches, creating diseases and various kinds of sicknesses.

One demon was assigned to just listen to what a person said and write everything down. As soon as a wrong confession came out of that person's mouth he would tell the others and they would begin taking things away. It appeared that what a person said could give some kind of legal right for the henchmen to gain authority or take something away from that person. They gave great attention to the words that came out of a persons mouth.

They seemed to be methodically killing, maiming and destroying each Christian. They were taking away time, energy, friends, family, jobs, wealth, health, possessions, etc. The head demon laughed as he clicked away on his counter.

"This is great," he said, "We are already up to one thousand things we have taken away today, and it is only ten o'clock in the morning." The demon let out a loud guffaw and put his hand up as one of his peers walked by. They gave each other a high fives and continued on with the task at hand.

The Fog

Demons were positioned to sit at the entry of the church and as people left they reached right inside of their head and snatched the Word of God out as they left the church to go home. It appeared as if these did not even know that it had happened. I heard people asking them if they enjoyed the service and saw them nodding their heads up and down. When they were asked about the preachers message was about they said it was good but could not remember what he had said. I saw them look puzzled for a moment and then without a further thought continued on with what they were doing.

"How can this be?" I shouted to the angel over the maddening noise that continued to get louder, "Do we not have authority over devils? Do we not have authority to trample on snakes and scorpions and to overcome all the power of the enemy and that nothing will harm us?" (Luke 10:20).

> 'Christians do have that authority' said the angel 'unless they give it up'. If you give place to the devil by not staying in relationship with God and obeying God's promises, you open up a door for the enemy to come in like a flood

"Christians do have that authority," replied the angel, "unless they give it up. If you give place to the devil by not staying in relationship with God and obeying God's promises, you open up a door for the enemy to come in like a flood," the angel responded. "If you only understood how ridiculously small and powerless these devils actually are, you would laugh and never give them another thought."

The angel held his hand up and touched his index finger to his thumb creating a circular shape. "This is how much real

The Angel and the Vision

power they have. They have to deceive, lie and blind your eyes to the truth in order to manufacture a pseudo power."

I surveyed the whole area and said, "Well, it sure seems like a flood has come in here, and it looks like they have done a good job of convincing a lot of people to listen to them. I didn't know it was this bad.

"What had we done to make the devil and his henchmen to look so much bigger than God? What a delusion and a lie," I thought while shaking my head. "Did not Jesus make a spectacle of Satan and his henchmen, parading them naked and ashamed with all their weapons on a pile for all to see? Should it not be big God, teeny, tiny Devil?"

Many of the devil's henchmen had paint boards in their hands. They were mixing up colors and were efficiently painting eyes and ears shut. You could hear them laughing and jeering with glee as they yelled back and forth. "I got another one. This one's not listening. This one does not want to believe," so he painted their eyes shut. Others were assigned to cut tendons on the backs of people's feet so they could not walk. As soon as people walked in disobedience or rebellion, little henchmen were running around nipping at the heels of unsuspecting Christians who stopped to dig in their heels against God's Word. Those who walked in pride, rebellion or rebellious ideas released a *spiritual ferine*. As soon as they dug their heels in, it gave the henchmen time to get a good cut on their heels. There were people all over the place just sitting on the ground doing nothing. They did not even seem to realize that they were rendered ineffective. They now seemed self absorbed and were whining and complaining to each other.

The Fog

This ferine agitated the henchmen, and stirred them up to a lustful, obnoxious, heightened state. It made them cocky and over confident. Encouraged by their behavior, they grew more tenacious and worked all the more harder. Before you knew it, people were wounded and giving all their attention to their hurts rather than the hurts of others and helping set them free. It was all about misdirection and diversion. Keep them focused on themselves.

The people were becoming numb and dumber from the pain. This numbness spread to their souls and had a paralyzing effect. "Wow," I murmured with astonishment. "I thought that when I was proud or rebellious that it was just an attitude. I didn't know it opened a door for the work of the enemy in such a powerful way. I didn't know I was giving up control to him. I didn't know it gave them the power to blind and paralyze me."

I saw boxes lined up all over the place. Kids, youth and adults were sitting down and they were watching and staring for hours at these boxes. A hideous little henchman was assigned to sit on top of the box and had a checklist in his hand. He was trying to make sure that all the bases were covered. I peered over the shoulder of the little creep and got a glance at the checklist and saw in bold writing,

Keep them occupied

Keep them from the One thing

"Something is very important here. What is the 'One thing'?" I wondered.

The Angel and the Vision

Other devils were assigned to reinforce what was seen on the boxes by whispering things in their ears. The end result was to brainwash its victims to be numb and dumber.

"Who would have thought?" I said to myself. The whole purpose was to distract, sidetrack and tie up people's time. The words, 'rebellion, side tracked, pride, wounded, not listening,' was ringing through my ears as I watched this unbelievable sight.

The air was thick with shame, guilt and condemnation. There was a strong sense of domination and a feeling that everyone was being forced and pushed to do things against their will. Yet I could see that people were making the choices themselves. Their pain drove them to fulfill unnatural desires of pleasure to numb the pain, and then to get more pleasure. They would repeat and do the same dumb thing over and over again. It was a cyclical thing that seemed to never stop. They felt obligated to fulfill their lusts. The boxes even cued you when to laugh and at what. Much of what was being encouraged to laugh at was coarse and vulgar. It was as if they were a puppet and their strings were being manipulated. They seemed to think that they did not measure up. Again, I shook my head as I found it hard to believe. I thought they were just some dumb attitudes. I never thought they gave such power to the enemy.

> *I thought that when I was proud or rebellious that it was just an attitude. I didn't know it opened a door for the work of the enemy in such a powerful way*

I noticed the devil's henchmen kept looking up at the clock on the wall. It read 11:58 PM. They seemed to have an anxious

The Fog

look on their faces, as if time was running out. They seemed to be on a mission and worked feverously to run the time off the clock. It was a mission to distract and destroy. However, the people sitting there did not seem to notice the time. They seemed to be self absorbed and concentrating on what pleased them and made them feel good. It was easier to live some other person's life and dream. One day seemed to run into another, which ran into another. "We'll get around to it tomorrow," seemed to be the common theme. They would then yawn, reposition the pillows on their couch, and look back at the boxes. I worked hard today. I deserve some time off. I need to relax.

I wondered what could be so fascinating about these boxes that people would spend thirty to forty hours a week just looking at them when there was so much to do. They would look and laugh and slap their leg like they were having a good time, but I noticed in this realm that although they were with a group of people who were also looking at these boxes, there was very little, if any interaction. I glanced at the boxes and noticed pictures on them. The graphics were astounding and life like. Just looking at it for a few minutes seemed to have a strong draw on their minds.

Even as I observed, it was like a tracker beam pulling hard on me. It did not make any logical sense, but just the few minutes of observation had been greatly alluring and attractive. I found myself wanting to sit down and relax. I just wanted to sit back, and let someone else live their life before me without me having to interact or be involved. I wanted to be entertained without having to think.

The Angel and the Vision

The one thing that seemed obvious was the importance of time. You could hear people saying how time was flying by so fast, yet it did not seem to concern them that in the spiritual realm they were wasting time and were not being fruitful. There seemed to be a lack of productivity and meaningful conversation. I looked at my watch. "Wow!" I said, "I thought that was just a few minutes, but an hour had just passed."

I turned from the boxes and saw an area where there were piles of letters on the floor. I wondered what that meant. I would find out later when I got to the boardroom.

The angel pointed out to me that when people are not filled with the Word and live in bitterness, they ended up vomiting on others. Words of hate, bitterness, anger, pride and selfishness are poured out upon others people. The vomit acted like a flesh eating acid. It created surface wounds at first, but when left unattended, would eventually cause deep wounds. Many had great wounds from harsh words or frivolous words said in jest. "I was only kidding," they said. The demons really seemed to enjoy that phrase.

> *Suddenly all the joking and jesting I indulged in seemed glaringly wrong*

The piles of letters on the floor were found to be worthless words spoken from idleness and jest. Blood edged the plastic letters, and I saw that when the words were spoken, they would slice the person with paper cut precision before falling onto the floor. They were hurtful, hateful words which did not heal, build up or edify. There was no life in them; there was only death. They were, however, powerful words that could hurt, cut, maim and destroy.

The Fog

I felt a deep conviction and soberness come over me like a heavy blanket. Suddenly, all the joking and jesting I indulged in seemed glaringly wrong. I looked around to catch sight of so many people with huge wounds on different parts of their body. They seemed to be suffering greatly. I noticed the wounds had dates stamped underneath them. Some of the dates were many years old, and were filled with a putrid puss and green ooze. Some of the wounds had my name next to them. Why was my name stamped next to that wound? On one of them the date was eight years old, "What an ugly, nasty wound," I thought disgustingly.

It suddenly occurred to me that I had said something eight years ago that hurt somebody and it had started to create gangrene in that spot. I had felt powerful and justified when I had said it but it had crushed the person I had said it too. That gash had never healed, and it had gotten more and more infected. Now, that person was in a life threatening position.

The enemy was busy prodding people to cause wounds in their brothers and sisters. No wonder the Word said to

> "Be self-controlled and alert, Your enemy the devil prowls around like a roaring lion looking for someone to devour."

(I Peter 5:8) NIV

Some people had so many wounds; you could not even see their arms, legs or even their head. They were a quivering blob of wounded flesh. You could hardly talk or touch them as they cried out in such pain and anguish. A word or look, intentional or unintentional would cripple them and send them into a tail spin. People were doing their best to tiptoe around these

The Angel and the Vision

people. A demon of suicide was guarding these anguished souls. I noticed on one, he kept combing his hair and whispering soothing, sweet thoughts of, "feeling sorry for himself and disillusionment. He kept saying that he needed to take care of himself now. He had spent too many years helping others and they didn't even appreciate him; after all he had done, they need to take care of him now."

My heart cried out to go and help lay hands on them; bring the healing touch of Jesus, to tell them this was all a lie; to tell them it was _all_ a lie!! My heart ached at what I saw. The angel pulled on my arm and said, "Come, there is more to see. We must leave this place for now."

The Fog

Notes

4

THE TREAD WHEEL

As I stumbled through the church auditorium, I reached out as if to push aside the wispy fog in front of me. I lifted my eyes and the air suddenly grew clear before me. Growing up we would host little mice or gerbils in a cage and would give them a tread wheel to occupy their time. It was a round cyclical contraption on a stand that looked like a miniature Ferris wheel. The difference was it was designed for its occupant to run around on the inside to occupy their time... Coming into plain view I saw not one but a number of these tread wheels. Although all of them were occupied but for some reason, I was drawn to a particular one. The difference this time, though, was that they were occupied by people.

On this particular one, a person was running at a steady gait. Sweat was glistening off his arms. He kept glancing at a wristband that monitored his heart rate. Everything about this individual was perfection. He wore expensive running gear and

The Angel and the Vision

top of the line shoes. He was very much focused, and was taking careful attention to the race he was running.

Off to the side, a foul little minion was cheering him on. "You're running a good race. Keep up the good work. Everything is under control. Don't change anything." He sounded really encouraging, and I could see that the individual thought he was on the right track. He seemed quite encouraged and worked all the harder. Everything was picture perfect, except for one thing; he was in a tread wheel. He was running inside of a wheel and was going nowhere.

The minion turned to one of his companions and chuckled, "He doesn't get it. If he really walked by faith and not by sight, that church couldn't hold the people and they would be on fire. Boy, we would really be in trouble then. I love it when people hold on to their religious traditions, and try to predictably follow God.

"We must keep them talking about God, but not intimately getting to know Him," the other one said as a slow wicked smile eased across his face. "Don't rock the boat. Rock a bye baby," he guffawed as he danced a little jig. He put his hands and arms in a cradling position and pretended he was rocking a baby to sleep. "Coochy, Coochy, coo. Christians are so easy to fool. If they only knew what we know they would be on fire." The two of them burst out cackling, rolling on the ground holding their sides in hysterical laughter. Get what I said, be on fire!"

The minions knew quite well that the tread wheel represented religious traditions without a personal relationship with God. Their job was to encourage 'Christians' to go through the motions. They were here to whisper in their ears that they should keep it safe.

The Tread wheel

I felt indignant and wondered who would be trying not to rock the boat and keep things comfortable or safe for that matter. Who would be listening to this garbage? It was so blatantly a lie. As I looked back at the tread wheel and the man's face came clearly into view, the blood drained completely from my own face. I suddenly was feeling very dizzy. I could not believe my eyes. It was ...**me**. It was me? What was I doing on that tread wheel? What was this all about?

> *The grotesque faces turned to look at me and I saw a shadow of my true self looking back at me. I saw a part of me in each of these faces*

A great confusion settled deep within me. For the last hour I thought I was looking at what was happening to others. Was I not the one who had compassion on others? Was I not the one who was concerned? As I stood there fuming in disbelief, I suddenly experienced a revelation and a series of flashbacks appeared before my eyes. The angel had just snapped his fingers and the lens had rotated silently. Abruptly, a clarity came over me, and I saw that the deformed people I had been witnessing were in reality, me. The grotesque faces turned to look at me, and I saw a shadow of my true self looking back at me. I saw a part of myself in each of these faces.

Here I was, with the seer's eyes and what I was seeing was in reality, myself. I was worshiping items of wood, plastic and metal. I was the one sitting and staring at the boxes for hours on end. I was the one that was disobedient and rebellious. It was me whose eyes and ears had been painted shut. A blank hollow stare was looking back at me, and I shuddered at the emptiness that peered back. I was staring into a sinister, dark hole of abyss, and it was a truly a deep, black hole.

The Angel and the Vision

I had been wounding and hurting others, and vomiting all over them for years. I had given my ears to the wrong voices, and it had crippled and deformed me. I stumbled backwards and fell, but kept pushing myself hard with my hands and back pedaling. My butt scooted across the floor as my legs flailed backwards in a panic as I tried to get as far away as possible.

This was horrifying, and I was terrified at what I had just seen. This true self was the only self I had ever known and I was fast learning that it was ugly.

The angel laid a hand on my shoulder and said quietly, "You are to be a living representation of Jesus. You must let the Spirit lead. God will not share His glory with anyone. You are His and His alone. The Lord sees you perfect and holy, but you are not living perfect and holy."

> I had no idea how to perform what the angel was asking.

I heard the angel continue to muse. "That is what Jesus had said."

My head pounded and felt like it was about to explode. There seemed to be such a contradiction between what the angel was saying about me, and what I was seeing about myself.

How could I be a living representation of Jesus when I looked and acted like this? A dull headache had begun to creep up the back of my neck and was creating a pulsating throb on my temples. I rubbed my eyes and sighed while heaviness that seemed to press down on me with great force. This was very painful. I sat down for a moment feeling very numb and confused. More importantly, I was mortified by what had

The Tread wheel

stared back at me from the abyss. I had no idea how to perform what the angel was asking.

My insides were hollow, and it felt like someone had just taken a blow torch and turned it on inside of me. I felt like I had been burned to a crisp. I began to cough and sneeze as the sulfuric ash of my soul transcended from a spiritual manifestation to a physical one. I tried to suck in a breath of fresh air, but found myself gasping for a breath of air but I seemed to be just breathing the foggy air that I was manifesting. I truly began to get physically sick.

I heard a voice say, "Are you being lead by the Spirit, or are you leading the Spirit".

To me it was obvious. I was leading the Spirit, and trying to push Him to fulfill my own agenda. I had determined what was godly. The obvious results were horrifying. This was the result of my own form of godliness. I let out a hollow cough again and held my sides. Lying on the ground, I pulled my legs up into a fetal position, and laid there as one who was dead. I just wished the pain and heartache would go away.

Notes

5

THE STORAGE ROOM

Eventually, I forced myself to get back on my feet. Shaking my head a stunned feeling settled over me as I remembered what I had just seen. I stumbled behind the angel following him from a short distance as he led me on to the next place.

As the fog around that area cleared, a door came into view titled 'Storage Room'.

"Open the door," the angel instructed, "and look inside".

As I opened the door and poked my head inside, I was confronted with piles and piles of Bibles. The dust was very thick on everything and caused me to sneeze three times very loudly. I put myself together and wiped my nose on a Kleenex as I squinted my eyes together in order to adjust to the dim interior. Looking around I found myself confronted by various pieces of armor. The Bibles seemed to have a translucent look

The Angel and the Vision

to them. In the spirit world they seemed to change from just looking like a book to a sword. It was kind of like those cards that you turn at a different angle, and they turn into something else. This was that same kind of picture.

"I have a feeling you are going to explain all this to me," I said with a puzzled look.

The angel spoke quickly and authoritatively in reply, "The Lord Jesus Christ, Son of the living God who came in the flesh says. You have forsaken my Word. This is the essence of a form of godliness. You have substituted my Word for other words and other teachings. You would rather listen to anything, including music as a substitute rather than seek my presence. You are wearing a cloak of religiousness, but you are not seeking me. You substitute things for my Word, and the things of this world have choked out the precious Word and that Word is the Lord."

God has given humans this World to enjoy, but you are just a pilgrim passing through

I shook my head in bewilderment at the directness of the angel. He certainly did not mince any words.

"Is the Lord saying that we should not listen to good and godly music or other messages or books?" I asked hesitantly. I was amazed that the angel was not angry or impatient with my questions. "

"True worship flows from the Word and your intimate relationship with God. If you are in the Word and in a relationship with the Lord Almighty, from there you will begin to have discernment about whether other words, songs or movements are for your spiritual benefit. The key is to know

The Storage Room

what promotes pride and rebellion and draws you away from Him. Encompass yourself with music and books that encourage and draw you into a deeper relationship with the Lord. It's not one or the other. It's whether one enhances a relationship with the other."

I began to think about what I filled my mind with when I had free time, or anytime for that matter. I was dismayed as I thought of the endless hours on TV and Internet that were wasted time...and movies that I had watched and had vexed me afterwards.

There were endless activities that had no other purpose other than to fulfill my own pleasures. "Is it wrong to fulfill my own pleasures?" I pondered reflectively.

God has given you this World to enjoy, but you are just a pilgrim passing through. This world is not your home. The angel spoke intuitively as if he understood my thoughts.

"It's all about relationship with Jesus," I thought. "If I make Him my passion then there will be things I won't want to do because I love Him."

I was feeling more and more conviction. Behind me you could hear demonic henchmen slithering and writhing around in an increasing frenzy. Their voices grew louder and louder,

"It's all legalism. Don't listen to him. You have a right to a good time. God doesn't really want you to be in the Bible all the time! He doesn't want you to be around Him all the time either! *Stop bothering Him!* Did He not give you this world to enjoy?"

The Angel and the Vision

The angel ignored the henchmen and said, "As you can see, we are in a war. It is time to put the armor back on and fight." The angel repeated himself again by saying, "God has given humans this world to enjoy, but you are a pilgrim passing through. This world is not your home. You must not look to the left or the right but keep your eyes from evil. You must remove everything that hinders you and become a skillful warrior. You need to get back into the Word. Your shield of faith and the sword of the spirit are weapons that you must become very skillful with. One is a defensive weapon and the other is an offensive one.

One person who is skillful can cause great damage to the enemy, but a church that is skillful can change a city or a country."

> *True worship flows from the Word and your intimate relationship with God.*

The angel pointed out how the demons were accusing so many people of putting everything else before God.

> "They honor Him with their lips but their heart is far from God," they said.

(Mathew 15:8) KJV

I noticed that there seemed to be a truth to this. It also dawned on me that even the demons quoted scripture. Of course their intention was to hurt people, not see them healed and delivered. If they could use scripture to manipulate, dominate and control, that suited them just fine. Much of what the demons said were laced with truth but their underlying intent was not to set people free but rather control and enslave

The Storage Room

them. They promised freedom but inflicted shame, blame and guilt.

Over all, people just seemed to be divided and distracted, and were giving God only a small fraction of their time I noticed that God's people were no longer being completely offensive in their warfare, but were becoming defensive and defenseless, and it had allowed the enemy to do what he wanted. "

Their defensive and offensive skills had become warped. Instead of properly using their defensive weapon of faith and their offensive weapon of the sword of the spirit, they were just being plain defensive in living in unbelief and offensive in both their words and in how they responded to others whose hurtful words were an offense against them.

This is the mayhem you see here and because of it, the demons are in control," the angel said resolutely.

There seemed to be a war about worship. I observed a battle of who was going to get our time and attention; of who was going to get our worship.

As I stood there, a thought occurred to me, "Where are the prophets? Shouldn't they be here helping people to see and fight in a time like this?"

I had already forgotten that this message was for me. I was already trying to shift focus and worry about what other people were doing or should be doing.

Despite my attempt to misdirect the responsibility towards myself, the answer was closer than I thought.

6

THE PROPHETS

We eventually left the storage room and continued to walk. In front of me appeared a large spacious jail cell. I thought it strange that there was a jail cell inside the sanctuary of the church. The door was open and there were no apparent demons guarding it or even present... I looked inside and saw a group of people lying on the floor with their hands handcuffed and duct tape on their mouths.

Off to one side was a big glass jar with a wide mouthed top. The cover was off and lying on the floor. Inside was an equal amount of grasshoppers as there were people in the cell. I asked the angel what this meant and he said perceptively,

"The grasshoppers symbolize what has happened to God's prophetic voice. If you put grasshoppers in a jar and put the lid on they will jump and try to get out. In trying to get out they will hit their heads on the lid. Eventually, they will give up. Even if you take the lid off at a later time, they will not try to jump out. They have grown discouraged and disillusioned.

The Angel and the Vision

I noticed an inscription etched on the hand cuffs. It said 'man's opinions, doubt and the fear of men'.

"These people that you see here are some of the prophetic voices. They have spoken God's Word, but have been beaten down by a form of godliness and a spirit of religion. They have grown discouraged and disillusioned. They could jump out if they so chose, but have allowed themselves to become captivated by their own discouragement. They have grown silent and accepted the status quo. In many places they are not even allowed to speak."

I noticed in the corner a pile of scrolls with seals on them. I walked over and began reading the seals on the outside. I noticed names, dates and places. I asked the angel why these piles of scrolls were here in the corner.

"They are God's revelatory Word to His people," he said decisively.

"But almost all of these have old dates on them," I replied.

"Yes, these are words that were never given because of fear, discouragement or just plain disobedience. They never reached their intended purpose." the angel said with a deep sigh.

I opened up one of the scrolls and read the word. The more I read the more my eyes opened up in surprise wonder.

"This is amazing stuff," I said. "This could free a lot of people. This is actually very encouraging."

I noticed one particular man slouched in the corner with his hat pulled down over most of his face. Somehow I felt drawn to him, and got down on my knees to look at his face. A hollow

The Prophets

stare looked back at me. I felt the need to comfort him but I suddenly jumped back as if I had seen a ghost. My heart was beating wildly as I stared back in disbelief. No wonder I felt drawn to him. He looked like me. He looked...like me!

The angel motioned to me. It was time to go. With great sadness, I followed, but kept looking back at the man in the hat. I felt a peculiar sensation deep in my stomach. He looked afraid. "Why was he so afraid? The energy around him seemed so dark and distant.

What kind of spirit could have caused him such damage?" I asked, as I pondered these disturbing events. Certainly the fear of man does bring a snare. They were bound by their own fear.

"Was that me there?" I felt very troubled as I left. Something was certainly not right here.

7

THE YOUTH ROOM

I began moving on to the next spot, trailing behind the angel. Looking off to one side, I saw a man with the top of his skull missing. I leaped back in fear. A demon was holding a wooden spoon, and was pouring ingredients into his brain while stirring and crooning, *"a little bit of dis, a little bit of dat."* When no one seemed to be looking he would reach inside his head with one hand and into his heart with the other and pull what appeared to be important words out of him.

"He can do that?" I shook my head profusely. I would never have believed it if I hadn't just seen it firsthand.

We passed by the infirmary while continuing to our next destination. I saw a large circle of henchmen standing shoulder to shoulder. Each had their hands draped over the other's shoulders and were huddled in a tight circle they wore names on their backs similar to what an athlete would have on his jersey. I looked closely adjusting my contacts so I could read their names—boredom, peer pressure, fears, lust, intimidation,

The Angel and the Vision

deception, distractions; they were just a few of the names I saw on there jerseys...

The demonic henchmen wore uniforms that looked like those that belonged to an umpire. The uniforms were black and white with the strips going vertical. They wore black shorts with white socks.

The angel brushed aside a number of the hideous little henchmen so I could see inside. Demons tumbled to the floor like bowling pins and started jumping back up while making a big squabble of indignation. I smirked at the ridiculousness of their bravado. The angel just ignored them as if they were some worthless chaff.

I squeezed my way through the rabble, and saw a whole group of bushel baskets facing upside down on the ground. I asked the angel what these minions were attempting to do. "Oh, they are keeping a tight circle around these baskets so no air can get in." I furrowed my brow and wondered why that mattered. Again, I was thinking with my head rather my spiritual understanding.

"So, what is this?" I finally asked, pointing expressively to the baskets lying upside down on the floor.

"This is the youth in the church," the angel said with deep affection. "Each basket represents an individual loved by the Father". I lifted up a basket and saw a tiny little pilot light. All around the pilot light was kindling wood piled up, but it was not on fire. These kids seemed to have let the world around them conform them to its mold. They had let boredom, peer pressure, friends, and intimidation influence them.

The Youth Room

Without the Word in their hearts and walking daily in the Spirit, their flame had been reduced to a pilot light. They had hidden their light under a bushel and are staying disconnected from the Word. They had let the world, friends and peer pressure, squeeze them into its mold, and their light has all but gone out. These kids were not seeing a power in the church that is greater than the power they are getting in the attractions from the world around them. They were huddled in a world of confusion and fear. They were not experiencing the 'air' of the Spirit.

I blinked quickly and flared my nose wide as I got down close and examined the baskets. There was a musky smelling perfume that came from the heart of most baskets. I turned to the Angel with a question mark in my eyes as to its significance.

> *They really are cowards when faced by an on-fire Christian filled with the Holy Spirit and the Word. When you begin to love one another unconditionally that really messes them up*

"They are attracted by the smell," the Angel whispered quietly to me, as he pointed a thumb in their direction. "Pride and rebellion puts off a smell in this arena that attracts these cowards like a dog in heat. They get really agitated and bold when they catch a whiff of this perfume. They are living from their own standard of truth...from what they *feel* is right!"

On closer look, I noticed that some wore the perfume lighter and some much stronger. The lighter perfume I saw represented a quiet rebellion and a "one up" attitude. It seemed there were more youth in this category than in the open rebellion category.

The Angel and the Vision

"They seem pretty normal to me," I quipped. "Aren't they just normal teens? Teens will be teens," I stated with a slight doubt in my voice. The longer I stood there the more uncertain I was becoming.

"The enemy knows that the future is the children. If a slight wind of the Holy Spirit were to get through, it might fan the little flame and a big fire would erupt. It would then spread from one area to another. They cannot afford to let this happen. So they are holding on for dear life," the angel said. "Look over here. This pilot light at one time started to get on fire. Look at the charred wood around it. Something happened here and then went back to a pilot light; the wood around them never got fully set on fire."

"If they but called out to the Lord..." the angel spoke tenderly. "They are hanging on so desperately to what they can see in the natural. They don't trust anyone let alone God. They think it is their brand of truth that will save them."

I was overtaken by great emotion as my mind traveled back to my own childhood and my teenage years. It seemed so much clearer to me now as I gazed as an outsider.

The angel stood motionless, also overwhelmed by the scene before him. He seemed lost in thought for a moment, but then perked up with much enthusiasm and said, "Let me give you a visual picture of what happens when one of these young people gets on fire. I mean when they really get touched by the love of God and passion is ignited."

Immediately, one of the bushel baskets was on fire. It was so intense that the flames were dancing blue. It then turned to an almost pure white color. The wood began to burn with an

The Youth Room

intense flame and ignited everything around it. The fire continued to burn hotter and hotter. The wood that was on the outside began an amazing change. Some pieces of wood jumped out of the fire and ran away smoking. Other pieces changed from wood to gold, silver and precious stones. These were the youth whose lives had been changed and saved. And not just a meaningless profession of faith, but a life changing experience that resulted in fullness and fruitfulness. They got saturated with a revelation of God's love and began to experience it. They grew bold and fearlessly proclaimed the goodness of God. The ones that jumped out were those who rejected the message of the gospel. They got offended or embarrassed at the Word and would have nothing to do with it.

> These youth saw that they needed each other and began to respond out of love and care for each other. They saw the need to be teachable and humble. They saw authority as a protection rather than a threat.

The ones that listened and responded to the gospel, on the other hand, were changed into something incorruptible and beautiful.

I watched as the fire spread from one basket to the other. It was a magnificent bonfire. Suddenly, arrows of fire shot out from the bonfire, and shot towards different cities. The arrows left a continuous trail of fire from the bonfire to its intended target. Suddenly, new bonfires started. It continued to grow and grow. I began to see the awesome potential of a life given wholly to Christ.

"If these young people can grasp the fullness and power of God in their life, it would change their world," I cried out with

The Angel and the Vision

great enthusiasm. "What a shame that the philosophy of many churches was that little fires were better that one big fire."

"The key here," the angel pointed out, "is to always stay in the fire. These youth saw that they needed each other and began to respond out of love and care for each other. They saw the need to be teachable and humble. They saw authority as a protection rather than a threat."

"What you see here," said the angel "is more prophetic than you think. The youth are starting to be bored with boredom and are looking for what really is real. The harvest is ready and the fields are already white".

I was so fascinated by what I was seeing in the spiritual realm. I never realized how busy the heavens were. Warfare had broken out over the church just over this vision. There was a huge swirling of activity.

"What if we actually started praying and fasting as a whole body," I thought. "That would create a huge commotion in the heavens.

I snapped back to attention, as the angel tugged at my arm. "We have one more place to go", the angel said. "You know, it only takes a 'Word' for the enemy to flee. They really are cowards when faced by an on-fire Christian filled with the Holy Spirit and the Word. When you begin to love one another unconditionally that really messes them up. They also really make a fuss when they hear "in the name of Jesus".

"So why do we not stop and get involved with these people we are seeing? Why am I not allowed to help?" I implored of the angel.

The Youth Room

"Do I really have to spell it out for you?" the angel responded firmly. "If you don't get it yet, you will soon."

8

THE INFIRMARY

We were on our way to the last stop when the angel directed me back to the infirmary.

"I didn't know we had a hospital in the Church," I queried.

The angel ignored me as we walked into the hospital room it seemed to be quite a flurry of activity. It seemed to have the most people in it of anywhere else we had been. At first there seemed to be only one entrance/exit. Then I noticed at the back, a door with an exit sign above it.

A large pile of medical supplies blocked the back door. The medical supplies just happened to be prescription drugs for the patients. I paused for a moment to read some the labels on the boxes.

"There had to be a least a hundred different brands," I whistled in a low tone. I lifted my eyes from where I was standing to take in everything I saw. Above the boxes was an exit sign which said in a bold red lettering, "Healed and delivered".

The Angel and the Vision

I asked the angel why the door was blocked with medical supplies.

"Well," the angel replied as he warmed up to the task, "fear, doubt and unbelief have settled in. These people have accepted the fact that their diseases are either from God and/or they have to live with it.

"They have accepted their fate in life, and are just trying to make the best of it. They keep saying that this must be God's will for them and they should make do with their lot in life. They are hoping God will heal them, and are weakly saying things like, "I believe God will heal me or I hope God will heal me."

I wondered what was wrong with that train of thought. It seemed pretty logical to me.

I noticed that many of the patients had literally moved into the hospital. It was no longer a temporary place, but a home sweet home of misery. The doctors and nurses worked feverously to make the patients comfortable.

The prescription drug counter off to the left was an immensely busy place. The air hung heavy in this area with a stale antiseptic smell. I grabbed one of the prescriptions from the tray and looked at it. On its side was typed in bold print *'doubt'*, another was *'fear'*, and another read *'unbelief'*.

"What are these doctors and nurses feeding these people?" I said in an angry voice while slamming the prescription containers down on the counter. A top popped off one and pills went flying everywhere.

The Infirmary

The doctors and nurses turned with a menacing look in their eyes, "Quiet, you don't want to wake up the patients and stop making messes!"

The angel looked at me with that knowing look in his eye. "Do you see what I mean; these are not really doctors and nurses. Remember, you are in a spiritual realm right now, and not the visible one you are used to living in."

My spidey senses were on full alert now and my eyes wide open and alarmed as I previewed the entire situation.

I mused to myself that doctors and nurses are good for those who have a hard time believing for God's healing. They do a tremendous amount of good. Doctors for the most part treat the disease, sickness, or accident, where Jesus, on the other hand, goes in and heals it. Compassion welled up within me. "This is not God's will," I thought. As I walked out the door I looked back and saw across the top of the door, "By my stripes you have been healed."

> *I was seeing first hand that my own refusal to pursue relationship with God opened me up to a whole other World that wanted to destroy and afflict me with all kinds of physical and spiritual diseases and sicknesses. I was seeing the consequences in my own life just by seeing what was happening in others.*

"Faith is the victory!" I cried out, hoping that the people would hear. "Believe and don't doubt. Jesus already healed you 2000 years ago."

I noticed that the people who were going into the infirmary were looking down, not up. A look of discouragement and resignation was on their faces.

The Angel and the Vision

"They do not know God's promises," I stated emphatically, "This is not good!"

How many of God's people, I wondered had been gently prompted by the Holy Spirit, the Word, or a friend, and they had resisted that correction. Then God had tried to get their attention in a stronger way through a dream or a vision. When they still refused to listen, they had opened themselves up and had been subjected to sickness and diseases by their own unbelief.

"We have the ability to choose what we think. Often though we do not reason through the consequences of what we think. Negative thoughts and sinful actions create a huge strain on the physical body. It results in the beginnings of decay and death. Left unattended the body would eventually break down in an area and manifest sickness and disease.

We are not seeing the everlasting goodness and mercy of God; how God wants to bless us.

He has provided our healing every time," I thought intensely as my heart churned within me.

"We run from it to do our own thing and get tied up in these lies. It is a fearful thing to fall into the hands of a living God. God is so gracious and merciful," I cried out to myself.

Under the new covenant all we have to do is repent of all of our sins and cry out to God in faith and He will heal us. Satan has no legal right to our bodies, emotions or even our heart for that matter. Oh, if we only got into the Word day and night so we would know the promises of God and how they belonged to us.

The Infirmary

I was seeing first hand that my own refusal to pursue relationship with God opened me up to a whole other world that wanted to destroy and afflict me with all kinds of physical and spiritual diseases and sicknesses. I was seeing the consequences in my own life just by seeing what was happening in others.

> *Satan has no legal right to our bodies, emotions or even our heart for that matter*

I was interrupted from my preoccupation as I saw a multitude of patients in the infirmary and how they were like sheep without a shepherd.

"There is just so much more of God that we need to know," I thought. Jesus came to give us life abundantly. Why were we holding onto sickness and disease as if it was part of our luggage?

I left with tears streaming down my face. This is so wrong. This is really a bad dream!!

9

THE WORSHIPPERS

We eventually stopped near the front of the church. The stage was full of microphones, amps, pianos, guitars, drums, bongos, and every other instrument imaginable. As I stood gazing at the equipment, I saw the worship team arriving. Most had just come from a hectic week of work.

As I watched the team assemble, the emphasis seemed to be more on technique than spirit; the bass runs more than the spiritual crescendos. It was quite amazing to see all this through a different spectrum. As I saw this in the spirit, the individual worshippers became transparent as if they were like glass water bottles. I thought the bottles were filled with water to the top until I looked closer.

> *They were not seeing themselves as full: full from living constantly in awareness of God's presence*

The Angel and the Vision

To my horror most of the worship team were only partially full or appeared to be totally empty. They were not full of worship but, were coming to practice to try to get filled up. Was that wrong? Something did not seem right here. It appeared to me that it was too late. Worship should be a daily practice not a weekend cram session. They were not seeing themselves as full from living consistently and constantly in awareness of God's presence. As I observed the practice, the words seemed hollow and unresponsive. I was puzzled why so few were wearing a spiritual mantel; that mantel which would signify the call of God on their life to lead as a worshipper, musician or a singer.

Many of the worshippers had song titles attached to their bodies. On closer inspection, I noticed that they were titles of country, rap, rock, soft rock. These worshippers had been saturating themselves in songs from bands that were anti-god. In fact, these songs spoke against God and His Word. The cores of their lyrics were saturated in self love. Now they were trying to change gears and sing songs that were about God and His Word.

> *They were not seeing themselves as full from living consistently and constantly in awareness of God's presence*

From my perspective, they were having a hard time changing gears. "Should they be trying to change gears," I thought?

I saw oil being poured on the gears so they could run more efficiently. On the container being poured out were the words 'pride' and 'rebellion'. I noticed that the titles and songs had foul spirits attached to them. They had specific assignments to create a desired effect.

The Worshippers

"Ahhhh!" I thought, "It is the spirit of the song that is the issue here, not necessarily the style of music. How would one know that the spirit of the song was right?"

I noticed some worshippers who had a call on their life, and lived all day and every day worshipping in God's presence. They had a different aura. They too had musical instruments embedded in their bodies. When they spoke or sang, the music flowed in intimate worship. For the first time I noticed ministering spirits attached to their worship. There was a Godly anointing there. The angels came from the instruments that were attached to the worshippers. "Did they live there?" I wondered. They angels would join in and sing when the worshipper opened his/her mouth in worship.

> *I watched as the angel gravitated towards one of the true worshippers. He began to glow and a smile overtook his face. I looked on in wonder that this angel was being rejuvenated by true worship. Spontaneous praise began to pour from his mouth as he joined the worshipper who was giving glory to God.*

There were others who were called, but had not spent intimate time with God; the music seemed to come out of their head. The instruments that were embedded in their bodies seemed detached. The music was not flowing from there. It was a head or fleshly music. The music they listened to throughout the week was anointed in pride and rebellion, and it filtered through. They tried to imitate the movements of their favorite bands. The music that was coming out of their head had a light to it, but was edged by darkness. It was as if darkness circled each note. You could see the notes through the light. The notes were different colors and upon closer inspection, were notes made out of stained glass windows. "What a contrast!" I uttered in amazement. The ones who

The Angel and the Vision

flowed in anointing, who wore their mantles, that music flowed as pure light...in it was no darkness at all.

Hearts were lifted up to God and sustained. There was an eternal meaning to it; a power and an intimacy that flowed from it. The joy of the Lord was on their faces. They had the sweet anointing presence of Jesus that was shining through.

The other music lifted up too, but then came crashing down, like eating a candy bar, which gave instant gratification, but soon bred discontent and depression. I saw both groups of people singing the same song, but a different spirit was attached to the same song depending on whose mouth it came from.

I was beginning to see that worship in the flesh brought quick highs and quicker lows. It appealed to the flesh and brought instant gratification. It knew how to manipulate the music to get a desired result. These worshippers were quick to peek out at the audience to see if their contribution was getting the desired attention. Their hearts were filled with self love.

Worshipping in the spirit under the calling of God brought a swelling of intimate love, faith, praise and thankfulness high into the very throne room of God and maintained that presence. God was glorified. I could visualize the worshippers with these really long hands reaching out and scooping up the audience and then presenting it to God.

As the church service started, the angel pointed out that a large group of people that had come had not come prepared. Many had not worshipped all week. There were black clouds of fog surrounding those who were not living in God's presence. A large majority of the worship team hadn't spent any time in

The Worshippers

the presence of the Lord either. Many of them had dark clouds of fog surrounding them too. The one or two anointed ones seemed to be sometimes dragged down by the others who were there by obligation or personal agenda.

Each side was hoping to get some inspiration from the singing. One of the demonic henchmen was whispering in one of the musician's ears to "crank it up. Imitate your favorite rock band. Who cares if you dominate?" The spirit of worship was a spirit of 'self', not one of glorifying Him (Jesus).

The angel interrupted my thoughts to point out and say, "You must be careful not to worship your worship. Worship is to be the anointing oil to prepare you for useful service."

I watched as the angel gravitated towards one of the true worshippers. He began to glow and a smile overtook his face. I looked on in wonder that this angel was being rejuvenated by true worship. Spontaneous praise began to pour from his mouth as he joined the worshipper who was giving glory to God.

> *You must be careful not to worship your worship*

I noticed that some of the worshippers were wearing hats. The hats looked like baseball hats. At the tip of the hat, a string came down in front of their eyes. The worshipper's object of worship hung off that string. The object of their worship filled their whole vision.

For some it was their expertise, for another it was his ability to sing, and for another it was their looks. They were caught up worshipping their worship. "Look at me, how well I sing, how well I play, how well I write; notice my sincerity; I am so

The Angel and the Vision

spiritual." The incense of it went up to heaven, as perverse incense. It was like a fly in the oil, and it spoiled it.

It was disconcerting to me that so much of the worship was scripted and manipulated to get a desired result. The angel had finished singing, and finally came over and tapped me on the shoulder and said, "Let's continue on. You will be learning more of what it means to be a true worshipper later; but for now, let's continue on, there is more to see."

The angel shifted his shoulders up as if loosening them up and let out a contented sigh. "That hit the spot," he said with a smile of satisfaction.

I left feeling aggravated by what I saw and yet, was intrigued that the angel seemed unruffled and was able to enter into spontaneous worship with the true worshippers.

Here, I was upset by the obvious mixture of worship and how it was messing everything up. The angel on the other hand, was smiling with deep satisfaction. What did he know that I didn't?

The Worshippers

Notes

10

THE BOARDROOM

"This is our final stop, but the most important," said the angel convincingly as we stopped in front of a large room with a long table and chairs in it. "Everything starts at the top. As the leaders go, so go the people. This is why the under shepherds are held to such a high accountability before God."

I looked inside to see the leaders of the local church. They were seated at a table in prayer. "Good," I said excitedly, "They are in prayer. This is very good." I began to get very pumped up.

> As the leaders go so go the people

The angel interrupted me by saying, "Look again. I think you need to adjust your contacts."

As I adjusted my eyes and peered closer, I felt the lens move to a new position and I was able to see in the spirit the prayers

The Angel and the Vision

that were arising to God. I noticed, however, that most of their prayers were not getting out of the room. I looked to the floor to see piles of words. Like the letters used on billboards, they were in disarray and scattered all over.

They were the prayers that never made it past the ceiling, but came crashing down to the floor. I remembered I had seen the same thing earlier in the main sanctuary.

"So many of the people's prayers are not being answered either," I reasoned intuitively. I remembered that in God's Word it says:

> "Whatever is not of faith is sin"

> (Romans 14:23) KJV

> "If I regard iniquity in my heart the Lord will not hear me."

> (Psalm 66:18) KJV

Could my continued doubt and unbelief be considered iniquity? Was I living in a spirit that was unwilling to forgive? Were we as a church living in a spirit that is unwilling to forgive? Were we fostering offenses, grumbling and complaining? Had this become a bent in our lives that was permanently kinked? Were there secret sins that were being lived in with only a cursory apology when committed but not from the intent to turn away from it? My mind was swirling in a million directions as these thoughts assailed me.

> *We have created our own morality to fit the theology that makes us comfortable*

The Boardroom

Some of the men were praying, but half asleep; others were praying intellectually, but not from their heart. Some were praying eloquent prayers but which sounded hollow and empty. Some were praying earnestly and some prayers were getting through because they were praying in faith and not doubting.

I noticed in the corner a huge pot on a stove in a small kitchenette. It looked like a pot that Mother used to cook in when she made big stews. The smell was absolutely delicious. It had a top on it, and was making a lot of noise. It sounded like it was at a boil and was about to overflow. As the pot banged, popped and stewed, I saw three men who were trying so hard to keep things under control. The whole pot at times seemed to jump by the force that was in it. It seemed to have a mind of its own, and have its own purposes.

The idea of things boiling over and making a mess everywhere seemed to be a great concern to these three men as they struggled to keep control of things. "The soup must be ladled out in measured amounts," one said convincingly to the other".

"The people cannot take too much at once, or it will be too much for them. Baby steps are all they can take," one of the men said wisely as he struggled with the lid as it jumped again and he tried valiantly to hold it down. One man was holding a ladle and was trying to fit it though the lid and catch a spoonful of soup that the other had just opened a crack.

"Not too much," another one said cautiously. "Just a little slurp."

One of the men at the table jerked up from his nap and gazed lazily over at the two struggling with the lid. After a brief

The Angel and the Vision

moment of casually observing the three and giving a deep yawn, he gave one last disinterested look and dozed back off to sleep.

I walked over to see what all the fuss was about. I mean it was only a pot—right? What really was all the fuss! I looked on the top of the cover and read in bold print; **POWER OF GOD**.

I was dumbfounded. "Why would anyone be trying to hold down the Power of God? Why were these men so concerned as to not let the Holy Spirit have unfettered access to move as He wished or as strong as He wished in His church? Why were they afraid of messes? Why not let the top off the pot and let the pot do what it wanted to do? It is His church, isn't it? Surely the fear of man brings a snare", I reasoned within myself.

> Believing in God's power and demonstrating God's power is two different things

The angel sensing my perplexity said plainly, "Throughout the centuries, when people don't understand God's power, they try to dissuade it. They say that what happened in the early church was a special time; it doesn't apply to us now. The church doesn't like messes. They like everything packaged neat and tidy. They have a hard time seeing faith as substance."

"But our Church believes in these things," I said. "They believe in God's power!"

"Believing in God's power and demonstrating God's power are two different things. If the church and yourself believed, why are there so many sick among you?" the angel said. "Why are people not growing and being fruitful, and why are the Lord's anointed ones leaving the church because they feel

The Boardroom

undernourished? Why do the sermons feel more like lectures and teachings rather than demonstrating an unction, anointing and a power that causes the listeners to leave changed and uplifted?"

I felt stung by these words as its truthfulness settled deep within me. "Truly, we had become apathetic," I thought. "We will believe God and His Word as long as it fits our comfort zone and theology. We have created our own morality to fit the theology that makes us comfortable. We are preaching messages that seem doctrinally sound, interesting, even entertaining, but within ten minutes of leaving the church you find that you can't remember a thing you heard, let alone be changed by what you heard."

"God is a faith God, not a need God. He is not moved by our need. God requires everything to be done in faith without doubting," the angel explained gravely, "You cannot live in faith if you are not in the Word day and night. If you do it out of a religious spirit, it will not have any fruit either. The church needs to stop looking at numbers (for that is the fear of man), and stop worrying about budgets. God will bring the increase by His Spirit. You need to seek Him with all your heart."

> *God is a faith God, not a need God.*

> *"But seek ye first the kingdom of God and His righteousness and all these things will be added unto you."*
>
> *(Mathew 6:33 KJV)*

As I turned to leave the boardroom, the three holding the pot looked up and stared at me. I took a double take. It was

The Angel and the Vision

the pastor and one of the elders, and who was the third one? Oh no, it was ....**me**?

Again I saw myself as one of those holding the lid on the pot. The impact of what I had just seen forced me to my knees.

Even though I was seeking the Lord, there was a part of me that was holding back. I saw it clearly now. I was praying for more power and asking for it; I was talking about it and yet, something inside was holding me back. I was having a hard time totally letting go and letting the power of God flow. I believed only what I could see. I was afraid to take risks and step out into the impossible. The light coming from my life was edged in darkness.

I believed only what I could see

"Why is that?" I wondered. Tears began to well up in my eyes. Little by little the layers of my vanity were being exposed. What was I to do?"

The Boardroom

Notes

11

A COMFORTABLE CHURCH

I rubbed my eyes as I left and shook my head in complete disbelief. I was among those who had fallen into a form of godliness. It was unbelievable! I was holding back and controlling God's power. It was so subtle.

"A form of godliness happens on many levels and hits us all from different angles," the angel pointed out bluntly. "It can happen over a period of time or in a few moments. That is why you must be on guard at all times, and examine yourself to make sure you are in the faith, this is why God's Word is so critical. The world, flesh and the devil never stop and they never rest. So why should you be any different? You can be so easily deceived,"

> *You cannot repent of what you do not know is wrong*

The Angel and the Vision

The angel was now speaking quite authoritatively. It was like he knew what he was talking about. It was like he had seen this over and over again over a long period of time.

We turned to leave, and it was at this point that the angel gripped me by the shoulder and said solemnly to me, "You know there are millions of churches over the centuries that have been in the same predicament that the church today is facing, and God addresses this in Revelation 3. They have become comfortable.

By now I had learned that if the angel gave a specific scripture, I had better check it out. I grabbed my Bible and began to read:

> "I know your deeds that you are neither cold nor hot. I wish you were either one or the other. So, because you are lukewarm—neither hot nor cold—I am about to spit you out of my mouth.

God is getting ready to reveal Himself to you in a whole new way that will forever change you

> You say, I am rich I have acquired wealth (I am comfortable and don't want things to change. I don't really want the Holy Spirit in charge of what I cannot control). <u>and I don't need a thing</u>. But you do not realize that you are wretched, pitiful, poor, blind and naked.

> I counsel you to buy from me gold refined in the fire, so you can become rich and white clothes to wear so you can cover your shameful nakedness and salve to put on your eyes so you can see. Those whom I love, I rebuke and discipline so be earnest, and repent.

A Comfortable Church

(Revelation 3:15-18) NIV

The angel continued to speak with much conviction, "The problem is that people want God in their life, but not too much. They want to have a concept of God, but live by sight. In other words, they want to live by what they see, touch, feel, smell and hear. They live in the now and want instant gratification. They do not know God's presence and have not experienced a power of godliness. This is why I have been referring to God as your Master. That is how you see Him. "

"Actually, you live afraid of Him rather than seeing Him as a loving heavenly father. And that is why I am here. I am here to tell you it's all or nothing. That is why I started showing you what is happening in the church, because that is already how you think. You see everything wrong with everyone else, but have a hard time seeing what's going on in you. You live in the present and are very attached to this world system around you."

> *I had always thought that I could play the middle and there would be minimal consequence*

"However, God is getting ready to reveal Himself to you in a whole new way that will forever change you. Already, you have begun to see that what you thought was in others is actually what is happening in you. This is the beginning of transformation for you. You cannot repent of what you do not know is wrong. There is a revelation of repentance happening in you right now. I can see it in your eyes."

"You are about to experience God's amazing love, and you will be radically changed forever. The demons are right to be nervous and to look at the clock. The time is getting near. They know what happens when one person gets a revelation so clear

The Angel and the Vision

of God's love and becomes free from the lies that enslaved them. Now, is the time; now, is the day of salvation. This salvation that I am going to point you towards is a lifestyle salvation, and not just a pinpoint salvation."

I had always thought that I could play the middle and there would be minimal consequence. I did not think that my stubbornness in holding back from God would open me up to this bottomless pit of terror. Suddenly, all or nothing didn't look so bad. I now saw that playing in the street meant that I would get run over by a semi of evil forces. There was no safe middle ground.

I began to see that this whole journey I had just taken inside my church was not an indictment on the church, but a revelation of the state of my heart. It was a genius strategy to show me my perceptions of the church because those were my pet peeves. The reality was that I was blind to my own short comings which were clouding the perception of my own pet peeves.

> *I began to see that this whole journey I had just taken inside my church was not an indictment on the church, but a revelation of the state of my heart*

"I am too complacent" I cried out, "I am not hot for God. I'm comfortable with going along with the flow and making everyone happy. I don't want to reach out into the miraculous, or believe things I cannot see and declare them as so, because I have a hard time trusting God. I really don't know you. Oh, I am wretched, pitiful, poor, blind and naked. I don't really care for the lost and dying. I don't even love myself, how could I begin to love others. I have no idea what it means to know God or be intimate with Him. What should I do?"

A Comfortable Church

I fell to my knees shedding bitter tears. Great sobs welled up within me.

The angel spoke in a calm, but steady voice "There can be no fullness with a form of godliness, and there can be no fruitfulness without fullness. Jesus asks for you to abide in Him and Him in you. He wants to have personal relationship with you. If that is what you want, then you can ask what you will and you will bear much fruit. But, you must yield it all and repent of your unbelief."

I asked the angel. "Where is Jesus? I have not seen Him at all up to this point."

The angel looked evenly at me and without flinching said, "That's because He is outside the door."

"He is outside the door!" I exclaimed in a panic. "What is He doing out there?"

"When you become lukewarm," the angel responded, "The love of the father is not in you. That is why if you continue to read about the church at Laodicea, you will notice that Jesus stands at the door and knocks. That word is for the Christians who deny God's power and love the world rather than be on fire for God. It is for those who think they have no need. They think everything is fine."

> *Without fullness There can be no with a form of godliness and there can be no fruitfulness without fullness*

> "Behold I stand at the door and knock. If anyone hears my voice (the true Jesus-Son of the living God) and opens the door I will come in and eat with him, and he with me."

> (Revelation 3:20) NIV

The Angel and the Vision

The Master says that if you do as He instructed the Israelites of old:

> "To humble yourselves and pray and seek God's face and turn from your wicked ways, He will hear from heaven and will forgive your sins and heal your land."
>
> (2 Chronicles 2:14) KJV

"Jesus is saying that if you have ears to hear and you will open the door of your heart, He will come in. He only comes in by invitation. He will come in and have relationship with you. He will commune with you and dine with you."

"In my hand is the sword of the Spirit which is the Word of God," the angel instructed, "if you will raise your hands in total willingness, and ask God to forgive you for giving lip service, I will pierce your heart with this sword---and a part of you will die (your old nature), but you will come alive (a new heart), and God will put a passion (endurance for suffering) in you, and you will become on fire. God will rain down His Spirit and put a new song in your heart, there will be new prophetic words put in your mouth. You life will totally change, you will come alive, and you will experience deep relationship with God."

> In the midst of what seemed like heavy discipline was a deep overwhelming sense of God's love and grace. He cares so much for us that he wants us to have the fullest and most complete life possible

I replied with deep anguish saying, "Yes Lord. Yes! Yes! Yes!" Although the angel was speaking to me, I knew that it was really the Lord speaking to my heart. As I raised my hands I declared

A Comfortable Church

solemnly, "May nothing be sacred? Put it all to the fire. You are saying hot or cold, and no sitting on the fence. Pierce my heart, O God, with your flaming sword. I recognize my need."

"I want everything you have for me, and I want to be a man of faith without doubting to do your will. I want to be filled with a passion and love for you and others. Whatever it means to know and experience your love that is what I want. If you want me to lay hands on the sick and guarantee their recovery based on your promises, I will. If you want me to preach, I will. If you want me to serve in any capacity, I am your humble servant to do your will. Forgive me for trying to put you in a box and repressing your power. Forgive me for letting the enemy have dominion over me. Forgive me for allowing my identity to be attached to these evil spirits. I renounce their attachment to me and send them to the foot of the cross. I want to see your church alive and on fire. I want you more than anything."

> *(God) will pierce your heart---and a part of you will die (your old nature) but you will come alive (a new heart) and God will put a passion in you and you will become on fire. God will rain down His Spirit and put a new song in your heart, there will be new words put in the prophets."*

I finally was beginning to see that it was not about 'doing' but about 'being'. It was about being, and then flowing out in 'doing'. It was in saying 'yes' to Jesus. It was about saying no to relationship with the world and yes to relationship with Jesus.

"I don't want a master, but a father," I cried out in desperation. I was fully committing myself to the love of the Lord to experience it with all my heart, soul and mind. Whatever he told me I was... that was it!!!

The Angel and the Vision

I could sense that my time for the moment was almost done with the angel. I asked him, "Who would ever believe such a fantastic story.

He said "Turn to Hebrews 13 in your Bible you have laying there." I reached for the Message Bible which was by my side. When I had reached the spot he said, "Now read the last few verses of chapter 12". I thought it strange that the angel had presented looking up the scripture that way. I had no idea what I was going to see, but when I read the following verses it confirmed even more to my heart that what I had seen was truly of God.

> "So don't turn a deaf ear to these gracious words. If those who ignored earthly warnings didn't get away with it, what will happen to us if we turn our backs on Heavenly warnings? His voice that time shook the earth to its foundations, this time—he's told us this quite plainly—He'll rock the heavens: "One last shaking, from top to bottom Stem to stern, "The phrase "one last shaking" means a thorough house cleaning, getting rid of all the **historical and religious junk** so that the unshakeable essentials_stand clear and Uncluttered." "Do you see what we've got? An unshakable kingdom! And do you see how thankful we must be? Not only thankful, but also brimming with worship, deeply reverent before God. For God is not an indifferent bystander. <u>He's actively cleaning house, torching all that needs to burn, and he won't quit until it's all cleansed. God himself is fire!</u>
>
> _(Hebrews 12:25-28) The Message

A Comfortable Church

"Torch it all, God!" I breathed prayerfully. I reread the letter to Laodicea in Revelation 3. I came to verse 19 which said:

> *"Those whom I love I rebuke and discipline. So be earnest, and repent. Here I am! I stand at the door and knock if anyone hears my voice and opens the door, I will come in and eat with him, and he with me. To him who overcomes, I will give the right to sit with me on my throne..."*

(Revelation 3:19) NIV

"Wow!" I thought. "God loves me and is patiently waiting for me to invite Him in. But He is a fire and will clean house. I want to be an over comer. I don't want Jesus just knocking on the outside of my door, I want God in my life at whatever cost. I want Him totally inside!"

12

A PIERCED HEART

As I stood there with my arms lifted high over my head, I waited expectantly for the sword to pierce my heart. Normally, I would have had my eyes closed to block out any unwanted images, but I was on holy ground and my eyes were transfixed and wide open. The sword seemed to intensify in its flame and holiness emanated from it.

My eyes widened to their furthest point as I watched the sword on a direct course for my heart. On the blade of the sword eyes appeared that rotated in all directions. There were four eyes on each side of the blade.

> *Pierce my heart, I said. I am willing to pay the cost no matter what the price*

"Fear not!" said the angel, "These are the eyes of the Lord. They are all seeing and search out the hearts of men to bring light into the darkness. These eyes will torch all that needs to burn. Everything that is wood, hay and stubble must go."

The Angel and the Vision

I turned away from the eyes for they were as pure light, and I could not bear to look. I knew I was undone and nothing would escape their scrutiny. I had committed myself to God's Word, and to God who I wanted in my life whatever the cost.

"Pierce my heart," I cried out in heart wrenching anguish. "I am willing to pay the cost no matter what the price." I stared incredulously as the blade started to enter my heart grimacing as I anticipated the immense pain, but to my great surprise, there was none.

In amazement, I caught a glimpse of the eyes. They were not angry or terrifying but eyes that were full of love, tenderness, goodness and kindness. The eyes had a clarity unseen before and radiated with unparalleled purity. I watched as the eyes disappeared into my chest and was amazed to see the eyes change from light to love.

> Because you are willing, this sword is able to easily penetrate your heart. Your heart is good soil. Do not fear for the Word of God is gracious and compassionate. You are a Son of God and He loves so dearly those he disciplines

The sword entered my heart easily and effortlessly. I stood there stupefied at 'the eyes'. Again, I could not help but observe that the eyes were not angry or terrifying. Subconsciously, I was expecting the worse, but now found myself dumbfounded. When I had first seen the eyes on the blade as pure light, I was expecting the worst, but they had entered my heart filled with love.

"But wasn't God going to clean house and burn up everything? Isn't He God and I man? Should I not I feel ashamed?" I whispered almost inaudibly. I rubbed my eyes hard and followed that by pressing my index finder deep into my temple rubbing hard.

A Pierced Heart

I felt like I should be bent over while waiting for the rod of correction; yes, waiting for the heavy blow of a father or mothers hand; waiting for the wrath and anger deserved because I had been bad.

This was somehow different though; they were eyes filled with love and compassion. I breathed in deeply and slowly although my heart was pounding like it was coming out of my chest.

I felt no shame or condemnation and it puzzled me. I couldn't help but say it over and over again. It was such a revelation to me. A sense of cautious relief melted over me.

"Because you are willing, this sword is able to easily penetrate your heart. Your heart is good soil. Do not fear for the Word of God is gracious and compassionate. You are a Son of God and He loves so dearly those He disciplines. This is a good and holy thing." The angel replied as he looked at me with a remarkable tenderness.

A great peace flooded my heart. I was no longer afraid as the eyes of the Lord began to look. "Anything bad has to go," I whispered quietly. A change of thought was already happening. It had started when I had looked into the precious eyes on the sword. Fear had been replaced with an accepting love. I felt so drawn to those eyes. Why had I been so afraid before? I got the feeling that my world was about to be rocked like never before, and I was actually OK with that.

"Would you like to see the inside of your heart?" the angel inquired curiously searching out my eyes to see what story it told?

The Angel and the Vision

"Yes, show me my heart," I replied excitedly. I rubbed my hands together in suspenseful expectation.

A panorama immediately unveiled itself before my eyes. I was in a twenty year old house, but it was really trashed on the inside. I say twenty year old house, because that was when I had truly asked Jesus to come into my heart. He had given me this new home, but I had not taken good care of it. In fact, I had let it get run over these past twenty years. Piles of trash and dirt were scattered everywhere.

All the rooms were in disarray and most were difficult to walk through. One room was completely filled with rank, smelling manure. Many rooms were locked and you could not enter in. A putrid, damp smell of mildew and moldy stale air permeated the air and tickled my senses. The walls of the house were severely damaged. Marks were on all the walls, but many were filled with holes. Some walls were totally black, as if there had been a fire. There were exposed studs on some walls that had been burned half way through. A majority of walls were covered with intricate stone work. It was like the kind you would see on a chimney, except the walls and ceilings were partially covered in stone.

Most of the rooms had a maze of brick walls running through them. The walls were at varied heights throughout the house. An empty mortar box was sitting as if waiting for the master mason to mix up a new batch and lay more brick.

Several empty bags of mortar mix lay on the ground. I looked at the name on the bag and furrowed my eyebrows into a question mark.

A Pierced Heart

"Selpridion," I mused with careful thought. I had never heard of that brand. I held the bag in my hand mulling over the brand name printed in bold ink across its face. I set down the empty bag and began to examine the intricate brickwork. Each brick and stone was stamped with some kind of past memory. I ran my fingers lightly over the stones trying to decipher their meaning but felt nothing, except the rough stony graininess of the rocks. The bricks were hard and looked like a loaf of bread that had been sitting around for too long and had become rock solid hard.

A dense fog seemed to permeate the entire house with a damp confusion. Somehow, I was allowed to see through the fog clearly, yet its presence was unmistakably real. It suddenly dawned on me that I had moved the contact lenses to a new position. This new position had given me the ability to have light vision. These contact lenses were amazing! My exuberance was short lived, though, as I snapped back to the present dungy feeling. I shivered involuntarily and pulled my arms across my chest to try and get warm. I found myself becoming sleepy and lacking in energy. As I walked through the hallway, I was able to see things remarkably clear, but yet felt a profound sense of deep shame, guilt and depression. "What a failure I am," I thought. "What's the use?"

> *They were eyes filled with love, tenderness, goodness and kindness*

Clutter was everywhere, but some rooms were only a small artery of a path to walk through. Stuff was piled (or thrown) everywhere and was three to four deep in areas.

"Am I in hell?" I queried. I found myself wondering what happened to the eyes on the sword that had entered my heart.

The Angel and the Vision

I had followed right behind them. I found myself confused thinking that wherever I was going should have been spic and span.

We finally found ourselves in another room. It was the front porch with glass windows on three sides and a storm door. This was technically part of the house but there was an exterior steel front door with locks on it that separated it from the main part of the house. Yes, it was a room alright, but it wreaked more of death and decay than a fun place to live.

Inside the front porch, three average looking, but strong men were attempting to clean things up. It looked to me to be a daunting task. To look at them was nothing special. If you tried to pick them out in a crowd at a later time you would be hard pressed to find them. They were working inside a six by six area that was marked by a brick wall. The wall was about four feet high and was in the shape of a circle. It had a small opening on one side which was facing and close to the side door. I knew immediately, that the wall had been built by someone or something to contain these men. But why?

Who had put these three men inside this little brick enclosure? And why did these three men not just pick a spot that was easier to clean where they were not bumping into each other?

They had small garden tools and small buckets to put the trash and dirt in to remove it from the house. The tools and buckets reminded one of what you would buy and give to a small child. To observe them, the job seemed overwhelming. They did not seem to be working very fast. One of the men had a notepad with two lines of writing on it. I wiggled my way closer in an attempt to look over his shoulder to see what was

A Pierced Heart

written. I stepped past some garbage and finally got a good position. I had to maneuver my hands on the top of the wall and lift myself up on my tip toes to get a good view. On the page was written.

> ** You have permission to speak to me between 10:00 and 11:30 AM on Sunday morning in church.*
>
> ** You have permission to speak to me and work in my life if I am in a fix and need your help.*

I paused for a moment with a concerned and perplexed look on my face. I got the sense that they were restricted to work only in this room, just in a certain way, and no more than at a certain time. I knew just by reading this that these were rules that I had set up. They were working off my instructions and wishes, but why the cramped conditions and four foot brick wall? The man with the notepad scribbled something on his notepad. It immediately dawned on me that this six foot by six foot area was the only area that they were allowed to work in, and my instructions that were written on the paper had everything to do with it.

The angel and I left the porch and moved to the center of the house. As we left, I wondered why the angel didn't tell me who these three men were.

In another room, which I guess you would call the living room, was this really large fat man who sat on a sofa gorging his face with all kinds of fast foods? He had a big drumstick in one hand and was tearing pieces of chicken off the bone. Grease dribbled off his chin and stained his big, fat belly. He was burping and belching out orders as he lazily slouched on the

The Angel and the Vision

couch. His big, fat tummy spilled out from under his frightfully stained t-shirt, and hung over the edge of the couch as he lay sideways all the while belching and burping.

Three rather menacing and mean looking friends were lounging on the sofa. These guys seemed to have pretty much unrestricted access to the whole house (except the one part of the front porch where other the three men were working), and they were creating mayhem and chaos.

As I stood there with the angel, one of the three individuals on the couch got up to lay some more bricks. A small bag of mortar mix had just arrived, and this person was busy mixing up a batch to lay another brick.

> Her goal is to weigh you down and make you cold and old. She wants to isolate you from others and make you hard as stone.

As I observed, I noticed that it was a woman.

"Who is that and what is she doing," I asked the angel, with an inquisitive tone.

"That is worldly Wendy. She is the master mason that you have allowed into your heart. She is the one that is creating all these walls and stonework. Over the years she has laid these bricks one stone at a time and is slowly changing your heart into a heart of stone. Your heart is your home, and this house is your heart."

"You supply the ingredients. Each stone is a memory where you accepted this world's system into your heart. Worldly Wendy is just waiting for you to supply her with 'selpridion' for your good and bad memories. You have repeatedly sought her out to fulfill your own lusts.

A Pierced Heart

"What you might not have realized, is that she also has an agenda. If you give her an inch she will take a mile. Her goal is to weigh you down and make you cold and old. She wants to isolate you from others and make you hard as stone. Do you see that mortar over there? That is the mortar that holds the good and bad memories together. Notice that many of the memories are still soft and pliable but when she mixes it with that mortar, eventually it will dry out and turn it to brick."

"Why is it called 'selpridion'?" I asked, with a profound sense of curiosity.

"Selpridion is a combination of self, pride and rebellion," the angel stated wisely.

"But, I just repented and asked the sword to penetrate my heart," I said with a slight confusion.

"Do you remember when you were younger at your grandparent's farm? Remember when you were auguring grain from the grain wagons into the bins in the barn?"

"Yes, I remember," I half smiled, as I remembered the bright orange grain wagons that had a sloped floor with a door at the bottom. As you opened the door, the grain would fall into a wooden box that was about four feet square and about eighteen inches high. An auger that was inside a circular steel sleeve with a motor attached was placed into the wooden box to suck up the grain. The end of the auger was placed high in the air just over the grain bins in the barn. I could still hear the swirling of wheat as it whisked up the auger and cascaded into the bins.

The Angel and the Vision

"What happens when you brushed the last bits of grain from the grain wagon into the wooden box, does it stop going into the grain bin in the barn?"

The light began to come on, as I visualized the picture. "No it doesn't," I responded with renewed enthusiasm. "There still is grain in the auger. It takes time for it to finish its course."

"That's the way it is in life," the angel instructed. "You reap what you sow and sometimes it takes time for the results to show up. This 'selpridion' is a result from several months ago concerning an event you experienced that you did not handle well."

I nodded my head in understanding. I guess it made sense. I turned back and meandered to the breezeway where the other three men that were working with the pails and shovels where slowly cleaning things up.

> Your heart is your home and this house is your heart.

"What does this mean? And who are these men?" I asked the angel curiously.

"This is your heart six weeks ago" the angel responded. "I wanted you to see what happens when you begin to have faith without doubting." He held up his hand, and we were immediately in the present.

"Wow," I thought. "Time seemed irrelevant in this place." A whole different sight was before me. The three men were still working, but the tools had changed. Instead of using a small garden shovel and a small pail to clean things up, they had power tools and wheelbarrows. I now noticed that the clean up was going immensely faster than expected. I overheard one of

A Pierced Heart

the men saying that with what used to take five or six years, could now be accomplished in six to eight weeks. The men were beaming from ear to ear, and kept giving high fives to each other.

"Your pursuit of faith without doubting and your total surrender to the Word of God, has released these workers to have bigger tools to work with," the angel pointed out. I noticed that the circular wall was now broken down, and they at this point had access to the whole front porch breezeway. The lock had been turned and the front door was now currently wide open.

As I watched these inconspicuous men, it seemed as if I knew them from somewhere, but I still could not yet place them. One of the men had his sleeves rolled up and sweat was glistening off his forehead. He looked vaguely familiar. He was cheerfully pushing a wheelbarrow and shoveling piles of manure into it so he could dispose of it outside to be burned.

> *He was cleaning up the junk from my life and was cheerful and joyful about it*

His clothes were covered with the manure he was cleaning up. He was a plain average man, but there was something about his countenance and eyes that drew you immediately to like him.

I asked the angel who He was.

"Oh!" he said proudly, "That's Emmanuel!" It took a moment for me to realize who this was. At first I felt embarrassed. I should have recognized Him immediately, but alas, I only knew about Him. Kind of like I know the president of

The Angel and the Vision

the United States of which I know many things, but we don't exactly hang out together. All my information about the president is third hand or speculation. I guess you could say I knew a lot about Emmanuel, but I didn't really know Him intimately.

Tears welled up in my eyes and I began to weep uncontrollably. For the first time in my life, I felt this real connection. Emmanuel was in my house! Yes! He was in my house...and working! Emmanuel was shoveling my manure! He was cleaning up the junk from my life and was cheerful and joyful about it! It was so hard to fathom.

I began to feel the first strands of relationship being woven. I stared incredulously at this situation and was finding it hard to think that I had held them to this small area on the front porch for twenty years, or at least most of it, and yet here they were and happy as a lark to be working in my house.

I reflected back on the many Christmas programs from my past and remembered that when they had announced the birth of Jesus, one of His names was to be called Emmanuel, which means "God is with us". (Mathew 1:23) "This was Him, wasn't it? God was here, and He was now visibly in me."

The angel gave an open hand gesture towards the three men and said, "Those are the eyes of the Lord you saw on my sword."

I stared in bewilderment and wonderment as I noticed the three men who seemed to work effortlessly together. It was if they were one person, yet you saw three different persons at work in you. Sometimes they laughed, and sometimes they cried. They really seemed to understand each other.

A Pierced Heart

"The other two workers names are "Comforter" and "Rhema", angel said warmly, his eyes shining brightly. As you have already noticed, they work together seamlessly. A light seemed to come on in my head, and I was energized as it began to dawn on me. These three men were here to actively work in my life. They were here to help me. I had never seen God like this before. This was a completely foreign concept of having somebody in my heart that had a passionate interest in the well being of my house and was willing to help me.

I remembered reading in John 14:24 where Jesus was talking to his disciples and promised to send the Comforter, who is the Holy Spirit. He would teach us everything, and remind us of everything Jesus had taught us.

I could hardly wait to see what these men were going to accomplish in my heart. It was as if I suddenly saw the importance of what they were doing. This truly was a new beginning. Little did I know that cleaning out my house/heart was only a very small part of their purpose for me; but all would be realized in good time.

Little by little, the entry became cleaned. All the junk was piled in a huge pile in the front yard to be burned. As the entry became clean, I found myself starting to hum under my breath and walk with a lighter step. Could it be related to the work taking place in my house?

For the first time in my life, I felt hope rising within. Was it really possible to see order brought to the chaos in my heart? Could my heart really become clean and in order? Could this house that represented my heart become a place where these three amazing guys could be at home without having to constantly clean? But why were they only in the front porch

The Angel and the Vision

working? Why had they not come into the main part of the house? I had unlocked and opened the door.

As I said this, I glance over at the steel exterior door and suddenly found my bottom jaw dropping wide open in disbelief. There was no handle or doorknob on the outside of the door. It was only on the inside. It began to dawn on me that it was I who had to open the door, which I had just done from the inside... They would not force themselves in. They were no like some SWAT team on TV that came and busted your door down with their boots, and even apart from that, my opening the door was not enough. I had to be the one who invited them in.

There had to be a verbal confession. I would find this to be a principle that would follow me through this whole process. I had to *confess* with my mouth and *believe* in my heart the Lord Jesus. I had choice and needed to exercise it.

> If you are willing and available, we will help you discover your identity and purpose

Excitement began to build within me. As it did, the house gave a shudder in expectation. These guys who had begun a good work in me would continue it forever. I looked over to Emmanuel, Comforter and Rhema and gave them and thumbs up and a nod as I spoke the word. Taking off their gloves, they brushed the dust off from their car harts and entered the front door to greet me.

Opening His arms, Emmanuel gave me a big bear hug and with a wide smile said, "Thank You for inviting us into your house. What can we do to help? We are so happy to be here."

A Pierced Heart

Taking a step back, but still having both hands on Emmanuel's shoulders, I Looked into Emmanuel's eyes with a stunned look.

"Did I hear you right?" I exclaimed wildly. "Did You guys just ask what You could do to help?"

Emmanuel slapped me on the shoulder and with a disarming smile replied, "This may sound crazy to you, but with Us all things are possible. If you are willing and available, We will help you discover your identity and purpose. We are the original architects and builders of this house you know!"

Emmanuel stood waiting for my response with his wide trademark like grin.

Without hesitation, I responded with much anticipation, "Come on in and make yourself at home!"

The journey from the heart of God to my heart had just begun. I was excited to see how my dwelling place would become a home for us. Having just put a face to the eyes on the sword, I was about to discover the greatest journey ever. I could hardly wait!

To be continued...

The Sequel is already available by the author or

Lulu Publishing.com

The Dwelling Place

By

John M Davidson